THE

Depression of Grief

COPING WITH YOUR SADNESS

AND KNOWING WHEN TO GET HELP

Also by Dr. Alan Wolfelt

Companioning the Bereaved: A Soulful Guide for Caregivers

Healing A Friend's Grieving Heart:
100 Practical Ideas for Helping Someone You Love Through Loss

The Mourner's Book of Hope: 30 Days of Inspiration

The Mourner's Book of Courage: 30 Days of Encouragement

Finding the Words: How to Talk to Children and Teens About Death

The Wilderness of Grief: Finding Your Way

And many others featured in the back of this book and
at www.centerforloss.com/bookstore

Companion
PRESS

Companion Press is dedicated to the education and support of
both the bereaved and bereavement caregivers. We believe that those
who companion the bereaved by walking with them as they journey in
grief have a wondrous opportunity: to help others embrace and
grow through grief—and to lead fuller, more deeply-lived lives
themselves because of this important ministry.

For a complete catalog and ordering information, write, call, or visit:

Companion Press
The Center for Loss and Life Transition
3735 Broken Bow Road | Fort Collins, CO 80526
(970) 226-6050 | www.centerforloss.com

THE

Depression of Grief

COPING WITH YOUR SADNESS
AND KNOWING WHEN TO GET HELP

ALAN D. WOLFELT, PH.D.

Companion
PRESS

An imprint of the Center for Loss and Life Transition
Fort Collins, Colorado

Companion Press is an imprint of the Center for Loss and Life Transition, 3735 Broken Bow Road, Fort Collins, Colorado 80526
(970) 226-6050

21 20 19 18 17 16 15 14 13   5 4 3 2 1

ISBN 978-1-61722-193-4

Contents

Introduction

In my thirty-plus years of "companioning" my fellow human beings in grief, I have come to believe that depression and its consequences are the most serious mental and spiritual health challenges society faces today. This thin volume is my humble attempt to explore a very large and complex problem simply and succinctly.

> "The word 'happiness'
> would lose its meaning
> if it were not balanced
> by sadness."
>
> — Carl Jung

On the surface, this might seem like an overwhelming goal. It might even seem presumptuous to attempt to sort out the immense complexities of depression in such a small book. However, I believe that this resource can be of great benefit to the millions of people struggling to cope with grief and depression.

I am hope-filled and optimistic as I begin this book. Why? Because I believe that grief is a spiritual, transformative journey that we who have suffered losses take so that we can come out of the dark and into the light.

As you will learn, I believe it is normal and necessary to experience reactive depression after a significant loss, especially the death of

someone loved. Depression lets us know when we are depleted and
hope-less. It signals us to suspend, to take a time-out and listen with
deliberate attention to what is happening in the depths of our souls.
When we heed this call to suspend, we learn about ourselves and
our need to mourn.

It was Scott Peck who observed that depression is often connected
to our inability to give up the old for the new. In large part, that is
what mourning is all about—giving
up aspects of a life we used to know
and adapting to the new and different.
After the death of someone loved,
this shift means slowly and painfully
moving from a relationship of presence
to a relationship of memory.

*"You cannot protect
yourself from
sadness without
protecting yourself
from happiness."*

— Jonathan Safran Foer

The very existence of depression
is what helps us understand and
appreciate joy. Just as there is no
light without darkness, there is no
happiness without unhappiness. In
the dark of night, you trust that the dawn will come. In the dark of
depression, you can also choose to hope and trust that happiness
will return.

So, if you are depressed, you are not weak, and there is nothing
to be ashamed of. You will learn in the pages that follow that
mourning is the "shared response to loss," or "grief gone public"—
and that mourning, like grief, is normal and necessary. You must
not keep your depression to yourself. You both need and deserve
human contact. Without it, your depression will deepen, and you
risk complete withdrawal from the world around you.

When you seek out helpers, I hope you will find the support of those who take the "companioning" approach I advocate for depression. Even if clinical depression or complicated grief are blocking your path to healing, I will still suggest that the spiritual-companioning philosophy, when used together with up-to-date medical understanding, provides the best approach to help you out of the darkness of depression and into the light of a new tomorrow.

A renewed sense of meaning, purpose, and, yes, even joy, await you. A deep harmony of mind, body, and spirit was yours at birth and can be yours again. Your openness to love and the capacity for wholeness is still within you. If deep depression has been part of your life for some time, you may believe it impossible to recapture your pre-depression self. But I assure you, it is possible, even probable. Starting right now, be proud yet humbled by your sincere intention and allow yourself to see even the slightest glimmer of light that every moment of your life invites. In other words, even in the face of your depression, love yourself.

> *"Who looks outside, dreams; who looks inside, awakes."*
>
> — Carl Jung

You may feel alone, questioning your existence, not liking who you are, and feeling as if there is no way out of your depression. Yet loving yourself means recognizing you, seeing you, and honoring you just as you are right now. Even when you are depressed, it is a privilege to be yourself. You have been given the opportunity to feel, to experience, to live life complete with all its challenges and its opportunities. In the midst of the pain of grief it is easy to forget this.

Yes, even in the face of loss, please remember: It is a gift to be alive, and just being born into this world is a privilege. Being able to give and receive love and mourn your life losses is part of the beauty of life. If you neglect to affirm the truth that "blessed are those who mourn," you insult the consciousness that gave you life.

I believe there is always hope, and I know that there is help. I hope we meet one day.

Alan D. Wolfelt

A SPECIAL NOTE TO FRIENDS AND FAMILY MEMBERS

You may be reading this book because you are concerned about a family member or close friend who has suffered a significant loss and seems very depressed. If so, please keep in mind that depression often results in withdrawal and feelings of helplessness. Many people who struggle with depression often think, "Nothing can help me...," and they also often lack the energy to get help for themselves. In fact, it is estimated that half of the people in North America who suffer from depression never seek help. Ironically, the biggest roadblock to getting help for depression is often depression itself.

One of the most important things you can do is speak to your family member or friend compassionately yet directly. Let the person you are concerned about know that you are more than willing to help her get the help she both needs and deserves. Your caring yet firm message, and perhaps your help in making and getting to the initial appointments, may well be what saves her.

Here are some additional thoughts and ideas that may help you help your loved one:

Take note. Obviously, you must recognize someone is

depressed before you can do anything to help. I invite you to read the formal criteria for clinical depression in Part 3 of this resource. However, I don't suggest you give the person you are concerned about a formal diagnosis. Rather, supportively inquire about the potential of depression and suggest the possibility of seeing a physician or grief counselor.

Support without solving. You are a friend or family member, not a therapist. Actively listen with concern and empathy. Remember—do not lecture or try to talk the person out of being depressed. It is not that simple, and this may actually result in resistance to your help and a worsening of the depression. Also, remember that people with depression sometimes invite you to be critical or to disagree with them. Because of increased irritability and agitation, they might criticize you more than they otherwise would. If the person you care about is depressed, you want to avoid being drawn into these kinds of fruitless battles.

Express your concern. When someone is depressed, they need the concern and care of loved ones. Depression may cause them to over-isolate themselves and even try to push you away. Even if your efforts don't seem to be appreciated, keep expressing your concern and willingness to be of support and help. The thought process of a depressed person can project feelings of helplessness and hopelessness. This means that you will want to be encouraging even in the face of their tendency to catastrophize and see the worst in everything. Don't give up as you try to be supportive. Remain encouraging and hopeful.

Be patient. Treatment for depression takes time and patience. When indicated, antidepressant medications usually require several weeks to start working. In addition, some depressions demand a search for the right medication that can take months of experimentation with different antidepressants. Counseling also takes time to help. Sometimes the initial counselor isn't the right match and the person you are supporting may need your help in locating a counselor who is a good fit. So, be patient and avoid the thought that the person actually wants to be depressed. While the depressed person may act in self-defeating ways, that does not mean the depression is desired.

Take good care of yourself. Supporting and encouraging a person who is depressed can be very draining physically, emotionally, and spiritually. Therefore, giving attention to your own needs is very important. Reach out for support and keep balance in your own life. You might want to see a counselor yourself to get the support that you need and deserve. If you do a better job of caring for the depressed person than you do of caring for yourself, you may well risk falling into your own depression. So, do connect, empathize, listen, and encourage the person who is depressed, but also attend to your own needs.

I hope this book will be informative and encouraging both to you and to the person who is depressed. Remember, action is the antidote to feelings of helplessness in the face of depression. Thank you for your love and concern for your family member or friend. You are helping him recapture life, loving, and living.

PART 1:

The journey we call grief

Grief is the simple word we use as shorthand for the very complex mixture of thoughts and feelings we experience after someone or something we are attached to is gone.

In other words, grief is the human response to loss. Grief is not something we choose or don't choose. Rather, it is in our wiring. It is the normal and necessary journey we embark on after something we have valued is no longer.

> "Death is not the greatest loss in life. The greatest loss is what dies inside us while we live."
>
> — Norman Cousins

If someone we love dies, we grieve.

If a beloved pet dies, we grieve.

If someone we love leaves us, we grieve.

If something we value is taken away from us, we grieve.

If circumstances we were comfortable with or attached to change, we grieve.

In general, the stronger the attachment was to the person or the thing, the stronger our grief will be.

You see, love and grief are two sides of the same precious coin. One does not—and cannot—exist without the other. They are the yin and yang of our lives. People sometimes say that grief is the price we pay for the joy of having loved.

This also means that grief is not a universal experience. While I wish it were, sadly it is not. Grief is predicated on our capacity to give and receive love. Some people choose not to become attached and so never grieve. If we allow ourselves the grace of love, however, we must allow ourselves the grace that is required to mourn.

GRIEF VERSUS MOURNING

What is mourning, then? If grief is the constellation of inner thoughts and feelings you experience when someone you love dies or leaves or something you care about is lost or changes, then mourning is the outward expression of that grief.

Mourning is grief expressed, or grief gone public. **I also like to define mourning as a series of spiritual awakenings, borne of the willingness to experience an authentic encounter with the pain surrounding the loss.**

You see, when you actively mourn, you create movement. Mourning puts your emotions in motion. I use the term "perturbation" to refer to this capacity to experience change and movement. To integrate grief, you must be touched by what you experience *and* you must express what you experience. If you do not allow yourself to be touched, on the other hand, or if you do not express what is touching you on the inside, you can't be changed by it. Instead, you will become "stuck."

You mourn when you talk about your loss, when you cry, when you journal, when you participate in a support group. When we experience loss, most of us grieve inside. But to heal and to go on

WHAT IS HEALING IN GRIEF?

To heal in grief is to integrate your grief into your self and to learn to continue your changed life with fullness and meaning. Experiencing a new and changed "wholeness" requires that you engage in the work of mourning. Healing doesn't just happen. And, contrary to what we sometimes believe, time alone does not heal all wounds. Mourning, which requires a time of *convalescence*…a very slow, gradual return to health after an injury, heals all wounds.

Healing is a holistic concept that embraces the physical, cognitive, emotional, social, and spiritual realms. Note that healing is not the same as *curing*, which is a medical term that means "remedying" or "correcting." You cannot remedy your grief, but you can reconcile it. You cannot correct your grief, but you can heal it.

to live and love fully until we die, we must also find the courage and fortitude to mourn.

DEATH AND OTHER LOSSES

If you have experienced attachment and love, you will experience grief when you lose what you love. You will naturally be depressed.

The discussion about sadness and depression in this book applies to grief caused by all types of losses. Whether your depression is the result of the death of someone loved, a divorce, a life-changing illness, a separation or estrangement, or even a significant life change such as a job loss or children leaving home, the teaching that I share in the chapters that follow is for you. You will find that I often refer to the grief of losing a loved one because that is the grief that most people seek help for. Yet other losses can also be very significant and naturally "depressing," so please know that no matter the nature of your loss, I am thinking of you and I mean to include you in my suggestions.

GRIEF IS NOT A DISEASE

You have probably already discovered that no "quick fix" exists for the pain you are enduring. This is actually a good thing. Because grief can make you feel "abnormal," attempting to return to "normal" life quickly after a loss can actually inhibit your rebirth. But I promise you that if you can think, feel, and see yourself as an active participant in your healing, you will experience a renewed sense of meaning and purpose in your life. Befriending grief rather than avoiding it dramatically influences its unfolding.

> *"Everyone who lives long enough to love deeply will experience great losses. Don't let fear of loss, or the losses themselves, take away your ability to enjoy the wonderful life that is yours."*
>
> — Barbara "Cutie" Cooper

Grief is not a disease. To be human means coming to know loss as part of your life. Many losses, or "little griefs," occur along life's path. And not all your losses are as painful as others; they do not always disconnect you from yourself. But the death of a person you have loved is likely to leave you feeling disconnected from both yourself and the outside world as well as a whole host of other symptoms. Remember…bereavement literally means "to be torn apart." Having the courage to slow down (in part, this is what sadness and depression invite you to do) and authentically mourn is ultimately what allows you to discover renewed life, living, and loving!

SYMPTOMS OF NORMAL GRIEF

When we think about what it feels like to grieve, we often think first of sadness.

When we think about what it feels like to feel depressed, we often think first of sadness.

Yet both grief and depression are more complex than that. To help you explore what grief looks and feels like, I have outlined some of the most common thoughts and feelings in the following pages. As you read through them, consider how your own thoughts and feelings compare. Learning about these normal symptoms of grief is about being self-supporting, not self-indulgent. In later chapters we will explore how these normal and necessary symptoms may be different in clinical depression or in complicated grief.

Shock, numbness, denial, and disbelief

"It feels like a dream," people in early grief often say. "I feel like I might wake up and none of this will have happened." They also say, "I was there, but yet I really wasn't. I managed to do what needed to be done, but I didn't feel a part of it."

Shock, numbness, and disbelief are nature's way of temporarily protecting you from the full reality of the loss. They help insulate you psychologically until you are more able to tolerate what you don't want to believe.

Especially in the beginning of your grief journey, your emotions need time to catch up with what your mind has been told. This mixture of shock, numbness, and disbelief acts as an anesthetic: The pain exists, but you may not experience it fully. Typically, a physiological component also accompanies feelings of shock. Your autonomic nervous system is affected and may cause heart palpitations, queasiness, stomach pain, and dizziness.

INTENTIONALLY NUMBING YOURSELF TO THE PAIN

When you experience a significant loss, you may be tempted
to quickly numb yourself to the pain. This desire to avoid and
to mask the hurt is understandable. But inappropriately or
indiscriminately using drugs and alcohol to help you do so only
brings temporary relief from a hurt that must ultimately be
embraced.

A well-meaning friend hands you a bottle of sleeping pills and
says, "Take one tonight. You need your sleep." Or you find
yourself sipping on the whiskey bottle to get through the day.

Should you take these drugs? First, never take prescription
drugs unless they were prescribed for you by a medical doctor.
One major study found that many people get their first
medication when they are in grief from well-meaning friends
and family. Don't do it! You don't know how you might react
to a certain medication.

Don't take a drug that your doctor has prescribed, either, unless
you understand and agree with the reasons for taking it and
the effects it will have on you. If you need more information
about why you are being told to take any kind of medication,
ASK!

Alcohol is yet another danger for grieving people. When you
drink, you may indeed feel better—temporarily. But alcohol
taken to mask painful feelings is only a crutch and may in
fact cause an entirely new set of problems. Psychological or
physical dependence can also be a problem with alcohol. If
you or anyone around you has concerns about your alcohol
consumption, get help from a trained chemical dependency
counselor immediately.

Drugs that make you feel numb or unnaturally peaceful will

only waylay you on your journey through grief. After all, they will eventually wear off, and when they do, you will still have to struggle with the pain.

Later in this book we will explore the circumstances in which medication may be appropriate for someone who is experiencing clinical depression or complicated or traumatic grief. You may, for example, become so exhausted from lack of sleep that temporary use of a sedative is warranted. And in some situations, tranquilizers—again, if prescribed by a physician—are appropriate for severe emotional reactions to trauma. Also, people who were taking antidepressants prior to a loss should continue taking them afterwards as ordered by a physician. But except in these cases, I strongly recommend staying away from drugs and alcohol as an antidote to the pain.

As you will come to understand as you read this book, learning to embrace the pain instead of denying or numbing it is what leads to healing. I know that it hurts. But you can and will transcend the hurt if you befriend it. Remember, mourning is a series of spiritual awakenings borne of the willingness to experience an authentic encounter with your pain.

Denial is one of the most misunderstood aspects of the grief journey. Temporarily, denial, like shock and numbness, is a great gift. It helps you survive. However, your denial should soften over time as you mourn and as you acknowledge, slowly and in doses, that the person you loved is truly dead. While denial is helpful—even necessary—early in your grief, ongoing denial clearly blocks the path to healing. If you cannot accept the reality of the death, you can never mourn it.

Disorganization, confusion, searching, and yearning

Perhaps the most isolating and frightening part of the journey through grief is the sense of disorganization, confusion, searching, and yearning that often comes with the loss. These feelings frequently arise when you begin to be confronted with the reality of the death.

You may express disorganization and confusion in your inability to complete tasks. You may start to do something but never finish. You may feel forgetful and ineffective, especially early in the morning and late at night, when fatigue and lethargy are most prominent.

You also may experience a restless searching for the person who has died. Yearning and preoccupation with memories can leave you feeling drained. You might even experience a shift in perception; other people may begin to look like the person in your life who died.

Other common experiences during this time include difficulties eating and sleeping. You may experience a loss of appetite or find yourself overeating. Even when you do eat, you may be unable to taste the food. Having trouble falling asleep and early morning awakening are also common experiences associated with this dimension of grief.

Anxiety, panic, and fear

Feelings of anxiety, panic, and fear also may be a part of your grief experience. You may ask yourself, "Am I going to be OK? Will I survive this?" These questions are natural. Your sense of security has been threatened, so you are naturally anxious.

A variety of thoughts and situations can increase your anxiety, panic, and fear. For example, you may be afraid of what the future holds or that you will experience other losses. You may be more aware of your own vulnerability or mortality, which can be scary. You may feel vulnerable, even unable to survive. You may feel panicky about your inability to concentrate. Financial problems can compound feelings of anxiety.

Anxiety and depression often go hand-in-hand. In fact, surveys show that 60 to 70 percent of people with depression also have anxiety, and half of people with anxiety also have significant depression. They are now thought by many psychologists to be two faces of one condition.

Explosive emotions

Anger, hate, blame, terror, resentment, rage, and jealousy are explosive emotions that may be a volatile yet natural part of your grief journey. It helps to understand that all these feelings are, at bottom, a form of protest. Protest emotions are often an instinctive reaction to get back what you wish you could get back.

> *"The primary cause of unhappiness is never the situation but your thoughts about it."*
>
> — Eckhart Tolle

Explosive emotions may surface at any time during the grief journey. You cry out in anguish, "How could this happen? This isn't fair! I hate this!" You may direct these emotions at the person who died or left, at friends and family members, at doctors, at people who haven't experienced loss, at God.

Unfortunately, our society doesn't understand how normal and necessary these feelings can be. The implicit message is that you should try to "keep it together." When you're raging or terrified, others may get upset. The intensity of your own emotions may even upset you.

Another problem is that people oversimplify explosive emotions by talking only about anger. Actually, you may experience a whole range of intense feelings such as those listed above. Underneath these emotions are usually feelings of pain, helplessness, fear, and hurt.

Just remember: explosive emotions are healthier (both emotionally and spiritually) than despair and resignation. Whereas protest challenges integrating the loss, despair cuts off integrating the loss. Explosive emotions may be frightening, but despair is deadening.

Guilt and regret

Guilt, regret, and self-blame are common and natural feelings after a loss. You may have a case of the "if-onlys": If only I had gotten him to the doctor sooner… If only I had been more kind… If only I hadn't said…

> "Anger is just anger. It isn't good. It isn't bad. It just is. What you do with it is what matters. It's like anything else. You can use it to build or to destroy. You just have to make the choice."
>
> — Jim Butcher

When you are grieving a death, it's natural to think about actions you could or could not have taken to prevent the death. But of course, you are not to blame. It's simply impossible to go through life in close relationships with other people without saying or doing something you later wish you could change.

Other potential aspects of guilt and regret, particularly after a death, include:

- **Survivor guilt**
  Sometimes being alive when someone you love has died can cause what's termed survivor guilt. Have you found yourself thinking, "How come he or she died and I survived?" This is a natural question. It may be a part of your grief experience. If it is, find someone who will be understanding and allow you to talk it out.

- **Relief-guilt**
  You may naturally feel relief if someone you love dies after a long period of illness and suffering. But your feelings of relief can also make you feel guilty. "I shouldn't be feeling relieved," you may think.

- **Joy-guilt**
  Like relief-guilt, joy-guilt is about thinking that happy feelings are bad at a time of loss. One day you might find yourself smiling or laughing at something, only to chastise yourself for having felt happy for a minute.

- **Magical thinking and guilt**
  At some point in your relationship, you may have thought, "I wish you would go away and leave me alone." Or, if the relationship was very difficult, you may even have had more direct thoughts about death ending the relationship. If so, you may now feel somehow responsible for the death. Know that all relationships have periods in which negative thoughts prevail. But your mind doesn't have the power to inflict death.

- **Longstanding personality factors and guilt**
  Some people have felt guilty their entire lives. I hope you're not one of them, but you may be. Why? Because some people

are taught early in life, typically during childhood, that they are responsible when something bad happens. When a loss occurs, it is just one more thing to feel guilty about.

Sadness and depression

You are likely reading this book because you are experiencing deep sadness (or someone you care about is). Sadness can be the most hurtful feeling on your journey through grief. We don't want to be sad. Sadness saps pleasure from our lives. Sadness makes us feel crummy. As Americans, our Constitution even says we have a right to life, liberty and "the pursuit of happiness."

But one of the fundamental truths I hope you take away from this book is this: **Sadness is a natural, authentic emotion after a loss.** Something or someone precious in your life is now gone. Of course you are sad. Of course you feel deep sorrow. Allowing yourself to feel your sadness is in large part what your journey toward healing is all about.

"We're taught to be ashamed of confusion, anger, fear, and sadness, and to me they're of equal value to happiness, excitement, and inspiration."

— Alanis Morissette

Even in normal, uncomplicated grief, it may take weeks, and often months, before you arrive at the full depth of your sorrow. The slowly growing nature of this awareness is good. You could not and should not try to tolerate all of your sadness at once. If you did, you could literally die of a broken heart.

You may find that certain times and circumstances make you sadder than others. Grieving people and my own experience tell me that weekends, holidays, family meals, and any kind of anniversary occasion can be especially hard. So can bedtime, waking up in the morning, awakening in the middle of the night, and arriving home to an empty house.

Have you experienced some or all of these grief symptoms so far on your journey? While I never encourage the comparing of grief, because each person's grief is unique and it's not helpful (or even possible) to determine whose grief is "worse," I *can* affirm that most people who grieve share many of these symptoms.

If you are grieving, your thoughts and feelings are normal and natural. You are not alone. And whether you are experiencing the normal sadness of grief or clinical depression, there is help and there is hope.

> *"Instead of seeing depression as a dysfunction, it is a functioning phenomenon. It stops you cold, sets you down, makes you damn miserable."*
>
> — James Hillman

CLEAN PAIN VERSUS DIRTY PAIN

"Clean pain" is the normal pain that follows difficult life experiences. "Dirty pain" is the damaging, multiplied pain we create when we catastrophize, judge ourselves, or allow ourselves to be judged by others. Dirty pain is the story we tell ourselves about the clean pain.

When someone we love dies, for example, we naturally experience grief. That is clean pain. But when we become frozen by worry that we did something wrong, or when we assume that others think badly of us (when in fact we don't really know what they think), or when we feel like we "should" be doing something differently than we are, we're experiencing dirty pain.

If you are struggling with depression, dirty pain might well be the culprit. A compassionate grief counselor can help you explore any dirty pain you might be experiencing and mourn your clean pain.

PART 2:

The sadness of grief

Sadness is a hallmark symptom of grief, which in turn is the consequence of losing something we care about. In this way you could say that sadness and love are inextricably linked.

> "In every heart there is an inner room, where we can hold our greatest treasures and our deepest pain."
>
> — Marianne Williamson

Yes, when you are grieving, it is normal to feel sad. I would even argue that it is necessary to feel sad.

But *why* is it necessary? Why does the emotion we call sadness have to exist at all? Couldn't we just move from loss to shock to acceptance without all that pain in the middle?

The answer is that sadness plays an essential role. It forces us to regroup—physically, cognitively, emotionally, socially, and spiritually. When we are sad, we instinctively turn inward. We withdraw. We slow down. It's as if our soul presses the pause button and says, "Whoa, whoa, whoaaa. Time out. I need to acknowledge what's happened here and really consider what I want to do next."

This very ability to consider our own existence is, in fact, what defines us as human beings. Unlike other animals, we are self-aware. And to be self-aware is to feel sadness but also joy and timeless love.

I sometimes call the necessary sadness of grief "sitting in your wound." When you sit in the wound of your grief, you surrender to it. You acquiesce to the instinct to slow down and turn inward. You allow yourself to appropriately, for a period of time, wallow in the pain. You shut the world out for a time so that, eventually, you have created space to let the world back in.

> *"But if somebody dies, if something happens to you, there is a normal process of depression, it is part of being human, and some people view it as a learning experience."*
>
> — Bob Geldof

THE DARK NIGHT OF THE SOUL

While grief affects all aspects of your life—your physical, cognitive, emotional, social, and spiritual selves, it is fundamentally a spiritual journey.

In grief, your understanding of who you are, why you are here, and whether or not life is worth living is challenged. A significant loss plunges you into what C.S. Lewis, Eckhart Tolle, and various Christian mystics have called "the dark night of the soul."

Life suddenly seems meaningless. Nothing makes sense. Everything you believed and held dear has been turned upside-down. The structure of your world collapses.

The dark night of the soul can be a long and very black night indeed. If you are struggling with depression after a loss, you are probably inhabiting that long, dark night. It is uncomfortable and scary. The pain of that place can seem intolerable, and yet the only way to emerge into the light of a new morning is to experience the night. As a wise person once observed, "Darkness is the chair upon which light sits."

THE NECESSITY OF STILLNESS

Many of the messages that people in grief are given contradict the need for stillness: "Carry on"; "Keep busy"; "I have someone for you to meet." Yet, the paradox for many grievers is that as they try to frantically move forward, they often lose their way.

Times of stillness are not anchored in a psychological need but in a spiritual necessity. A lack of stillness hastens confusion and disorientation and results in a waning of the spirit. If you do not rest in stillness for a time, you cannot and will not find your way out of the wilderness of grief.

> *"A pearl is a beautiful thing that is produced by an injured life. It is the tear [that results] from the injury of the oyster. The treasure of our being in this world is also produced by an injured life. If we had not been wounded, if we had not been injured, then we will not produce the pearl."*
>
> — Stephan Hoeller

Stillness allows for the transition from "soul work" to "spirit work." According to the groundbreaking thinking of psychologist Carl Jung, "soul work" is the downward movement of the psyche. It is the willingness to connect with what is dark, deep, and not necessarily pleasant. "Spirit work," on the other hand, involves the upward, ascending movement of the psyche. It is during spirit work that you find renewed meaning and joy in life.

Soul work comes before spirit work. Soul work lays the ground for spirit work. The spirit cannot ascend until the soul first descends. The withdrawal, slowing down, and stillness of sadness create the conditions necessary for soul work.

> *"I've had some dark nights of the soul, of course, but giving in to depression would be a sellout, a defeat."*
> — Christopher Hitchens

LIMINAL SPACE

Sadness lives in liminal space. *"Limina"* is the Latin word for threshold, the space betwixt and between. When you are in liminal space, you are not busily and unthinkingly going about your daily life. Neither are you living from a place of assuredness about your relationships and beliefs. Instead, you are unsettled. Both your mindless daily routine and your core beliefs have been shaken, forcing you to reconsider who you are, why you're here, and what life means.

> *"Everything is gestation and then bringing forth."*
> — Rainer Maria Rilke

It's uncomfortable being in liminal space, but that's where sadness takes you. Without sadness, you wouldn't go there. But it is only in liminal space that you can reconstruct your shattered worldview and reemerge as the transformed you that is ready to live and love fully again.

SADNESS AND EMPATHY

Another evolutionary and still relevant reason for sadness is that it
alerts others to the thoughts and feelings that are inside you. We all
know what someone who is sad looks like. His posture is slumped.
He moves slowly. His eyes and mouth droop. Being able to read
others' sadness is useful because it gives us a chance to reach out
and support them.

In centuries past we intentionally made our sadness more evident as
a signal for others to support us. We wore black for a year, and we
donned black armbands. We literally wore our hearts on our sleeves.

Sadness elicits empathy—which is a close cousin to love. Empathy
and love are the glue of human connection. And human connection
is what makes life worth living.

Receiving and accepting support
from others is an essential need of
mourning—one we'll talk more about
later in this book. If you try to deny or
hide your sadness, you are closing a
door that leads to healing.

> *"Depression opens
> the door to beauty
> of some kind."*
> — James Hillman

YOUR DIVINE SPARK

Your spiritual self is who you are deep
inside—your innermost essence, stripped of all the external trappings
of your life. It is who you were before you took on your earthly form,
and it is who you will continue to be after you leave it.

It is your soul, or "divine spark"—what Meister Eckhart described
as "that which gives depth and purpose to our living." It is the still,
small voice inside of you.

When you are grieving, your divine spark struggles like a candle in the wind. Many hundreds of people in grief have said to me variations on "I feel so hopeless" or "I am not sure I can go on living." Like yours, the losses that have touched their lives have naturally muted, if not extinguished, their divine sparks.

When you are depressed, you no longer feel the warm glow of your divine spark inside you. Instead, everything feels dark and cold. The way to relight your divine spark is to turn inward and give your pain the attention it needs and deserves.

> *"When we experience a loss, a hole opens up inside of us. It is almost as if the loss itself plows right through us, leaving us gasping for air."*
>
> — Rabbi David Wolpe

HONORING YOUR PAIN

From my own experiences with loss as well as those of thousands of grieving people I have companioned over the years, I have learned that you cannot go around the pain of your grief.

Instead, you must open to the pain. You must acknowledge the inevitability of the pain. You must gently embrace the pain. You must honor the pain.

"What?" you naturally protest. "Honor the pain?" As crazy as it may sound, your pain is the key that opens your heart and ushers you on your way to healing.

Honoring means recognizing the value of and respecting. It is not instinctive to see grief and the need to openly mourn as something to honor; yet the capacity to love requires the necessity to mourn. To honor your grief is not self-destructive or harmful: it is self-sustaining and life giving.

Yet you have probably been taught that pain and sadness are indications that something is wrong and that you should find ways to alleviate the pain. In our culture, pain and feelings of loss are experiences most people try to avoid. Why? Because the role of pain and suffering is misunderstood. Normal thoughts and feelings after a loss are often seen as unnecessary and inappropriate.

Unfortunately, our culture has an unwritten rule that says while physical illness is usually beyond your control, emotional distress is your fault. In other words, some people think you should be able to "control" or subdue your feelings of sadness. Nothing could be further from the truth. Your sadness is a symptom of your wound. Just as physical wounds require attention, so do emotional wounds.

Paradoxically, the only way to lessen your pain is to move toward it, not away from it. Moving toward your sadness is not easy to do. Every time you admit to feeling sad, people around you may say things like, "Oh, don't be sad" or "Get a hold of yourself" or "Just think about what you have to be thankful for." Comments like these hinder, not help, your healing. If your heart and soul are prevented from feeling the sadness, odds are your body may be harmed in the process. Your grief is the result of an injury to your spirit. Now you must attend to your injury.

You will learn over time that the pain of your grief will keep trying to get your attention until you have the courage to gently, and in small doses, open to its presence. The alternative—denying or suppressing your pain—is in fact more painful. I have learned that the pain that surrounds the *closed* heart of grief is the pain of living against yourself, the pain of denying how the loss changes you, the pain of feeling alone and isolated—unable to openly mourn, unable to love and be loved by those around you.

MAKING GRIEF YOUR FRIEND

Denying your grief, running from it, or minimizing it only seems to make it more confusing and overwhelming. To eventually lessen your hurt, you must first embrace it. As strange as it may seem, you must make it your friend.

When I reflect on making grief my friend, I think about my father. Sometimes when I fully acknowledge that I'll never see my father physically on this earth again, I am engulfed by an overwhelming sadness. Then I, with intention, try to give attention to what comes next. Yes, I feel his absence, but I also feel his presence. I realize that while my father has been dead for many years, my love and admiration for him have continued to grow. With every day that passes, the love I have for my father grows larger, undeterred by the loss of his physical presence. My intention has been, and continues to be, to honor his presence, while acknowledging his absence. The beauty of this is that even while I embrace and mourn my sadness, I can continue to love.

DOSING YOUR PAIN

While pain and sadness are normal and necessary components of grief, I want to make sure you also understand that you cannot and should not try to embrace the pain of your grief all at once. If you were to feel it all at once, you could not survive. Instead, you must allow yourself to "dose" the pain—feel it in small waves then allow it to retreat until you are ready for the next wave.

To ignore your true feelings is to become dead while you are alive. Instead, you can choose to allow yourself to remain open to the pain, which, in large part, honors the love you feel for the person who has died. As an ancient Hebrew sage observed, "If you want life, you must expect suffering." Paradoxically, it is gathering the courage to move toward the pain that ultimately leads to the healing of your wounded heart. Your integrity is engaged by your feelings and the commitment you make to honor the truth in them.

I encourage you to be present to your multitude of thoughts and feelings, to "be with" them, for they contain the truth you are searching for, the energy you may be lacking, and the unfolding of your healing. Oh, and keep in mind, you will need *all* of your thoughts and feelings to lead you there, not just the feelings you judge acceptable. For it is in being honest with yourself that you find your way through the wilderness and identify the places that need to be healed.

> *"To suppress the grief, the pain, is to condemn oneself to a living death. Living fully means feeling fully; it means being completely one with what you are experiencing and not holding it at arm's length."*
>
> — Philip Kapleau

Yes, the sadness, depression, and pain of loss are essential experiences in life. You are reading this book because you are feeling this and are struggling with the depression. Acknowledging that depression in grief is normal and necessary—even if the people and the culture around you are telling you that you don't have to feel depressed, that there are ways around the pain— is one significant step on the pathway to healing. The next step is understanding if your depression may be what is called "clinical depression" and, if so, having the courage and self-compassion to seek help.

AN IMPORTANT WARNING

In other books, magazine articles, and websites, you may run across a philosophy (and even "studies") that purports that humans are resilient and do not need to express their grief or receive support for it. The "new science of grief," as it is sometimes called, essentially claims that people "get over" grief on their own, over time, and that grief naturally heals itself.

Horsefeathers! Scientific findings cannot measure a soul-based experience that is not easily measured. Moreover, scientific research on grief may well reinforce our culture's desire to avoid grief and depression instead of befriending them.

I find it interesting that the same medical establishment that is promoting "the new science of grief" simultaneously champions the medicalization of depression. How can we "get over" our grief on our own, without any expression or support, yet need therapy and often antidepressants for our depression? It's contradictory, oxymoronic thinking that (as you can tell) not only irks me but further harms the millions of people who are hurting and need help.

If you are reading this book, you are among those who are hurting (or someone you care about is). You do need to mourn your grief to heal it, and you do need and deserve the love and care of others along the way, including, at times, the lifeline of a grief support group and the companionship of a skilled grief counselor. To mourn is to find your way back to a life of joy and love.

PART 3:

Grief depression or clinical depression?

As previously emphasized, it is normal and necessary to be sad after a loss. It is normal and necessary to feel clean pain. It is normal and necessary to turn inward when the world outside of us no longer seems to be charged with meaning and purpose.

In other words, it is normal and necessary to experience depression after loss.

The tricky thing about depression, however, is that while it is a normal and necessary experience on the road to healing, it can sometimes be disabling enough to qualify as clinical depression—and clinical depression will block the path to healing.

> *"Depression is the most unpleasant thing I have ever experienced.... It is that absence of being able to envisage that you will ever be cheerful again. The absence of hope. That very deadened feeling, which is so very different from feeling sad. Sad hurts, but it's a healthy feeling. It is a necessary thing to feel. Depression is very different."*
>
> — J.K. Rowling

Yes, depression has the capacity to propel the mourner to insights that can result in eventual renewal. Honoring the spirit and soul is about being honest about the sting of grief and acknowledging the reality of the depth of the loss. At the same time, years of research have revealed that clinical depression is a true medical disorder—an illness with a biological basis that is often worsened by psychological and social stress. We could say it has a "life of its own."

In this chapter I will approach this conundrum from a few different angles.

WHAT IS CLINICAL DEPRESSION?

As you consider whether you may be experiencing clinical depression, keep in mind that it is very common. According to the Centers for Disease Control, at any given time one in ten American adults is clinically depressed, and one in 25 meets the criteria for major depression. In fact, throughout their lifetimes, one-fourth of all Americans will experience at least one episode of depression. This makes depression one of the most mainstream medical problems in the United States. And, I might add, spiritually challenging!

Are these numbers falsely inflated by the swing toward medicalization of normal existential troubles? Perhaps. But while I worry that we are diagnosing clinical depression too liberally because we as a culture misunderstand the role of pain and suffering, I am not a depression denier. I do believe that clinical depression is a real physical disorder that sometimes requires medical treatment.

A number of influences can play a role in the development of clinical depression, including genetics, stress (such as a significant loss!), and changes in body and brain function. Many people with clinical depression have low levels of certain brain chemicals and slower cellular activity in parts of the brain that control mood, appetite, sleep, and other functions.

According to the National Institute of Mental Health (NIMH), symptoms of clinical depression may include the following:

- Difficulty concentrating, remembering details, and making decisions

- Fatigue and decreased energy

- Feelings of guilt, worthlessness, and/or helplessness

- Feelings of hopelessness and/or pessimism

- Insomnia, early-morning wakefulness, or excessive sleeping

- Irritability, restlessness

- Loss of interest in activities or hobbies once pleasurable, including sex

- Overeating or appetite loss

- Persistent aches or pains, headaches, cramps, or digestive problems that do not ease even with treatment

- Persistent sad, anxious, or "empty" feelings

- Thoughts of suicide, suicide attempts

The NIMH symptoms list is for depressed people and friends and family members who are trying to figure out if someone might be clinically depressed. In other words, it was written for lay people. The resource that professional therapists turn to in making a diagnosis is called the *Diagnostic and Statistical Manual of Mental Disorders* (called the DSM for short), published by the American Psychiatric Association. It is more detailed and particular in its criteria. According to the most recent edition, the DSM-5, a Major Depressive Episode

can be diagnosed when five (or more) of the following symptoms
a) represent a change from previous functioning *and* b) have been
present for at least two weeks:

1. Depressed mood most of the day, nearly every day

2. Little pleasure in all or most activities

3. Significant weight loss or gain

4. Insomnia or sleeping too much

5. Physical agitation or lethargy

6. Fatigue or loss of energy

7. Feelings of worthlessness or excessive guilt

8. Inability to think or concentrate

9. Recurring thoughts of death or suicide

Symptom numbers 1 and/or 2 must be present for the depression
to be considered a Major Depressive Episode, as well as at least four
or five additional symptoms on the list above. (Also see the note on
pages 37-38 about the DSM's distinction between grief and clinical
depression.) Major Depressive Episodes, or MDEs, are just one type
of depression that can be diagnosed by professionals with the aid of
the DSM. The others are listed in this book on pages 38-40.

> *"Here is the tragedy: when you are the victim of depression, not
> only do you feel utterly helpless and abandoned by the world,
> you also know that very few people can understand, or even
> begin to believe, that life can be this painful."*
>
> — Giles Andreae

GRIEF OR CLINICAL DEPRESSION?

In many ways, depression and grief are alike. We have already reviewed the common symptoms of grief (pages 11-19). Did you notice that most of the normal grief symptoms are mentioned in the above lists of depression symptoms as well?

> "That's the thing about depression: A human being can survive almost anything, as long as she sees the end in sight. But depression is so insidious, and it compounds daily, that it's impossible to ever see the end. The fog is like a cage without a key."
>
> — Elizabeth Wurtzel

Trying to tease apart what is clinical depression and what is normal, uncomplicated grief (we'll talk about complicated grief a little later) can feel like splitting hairs. However, the chart on the next page may help. Place a checkmark next to the symptoms that you believe apply to you.

One area to pay particular attention to is feelings of self-worth. While people who are grieving a death often feel guilty over some aspect of the relationship or the circumstances of the death and/or experience a temporary drop in self-esteem, they do not typically feel chronically worthless. In other words, people with grief depression may feel guilty and even hopeless for a while, but people with clinical depression often experience an ongoing hopelessness and low sense of self-worth.

Another way to think about the difference between grief and depression is to consider *how long the feelings last and to what extent your daily activities are impaired.* Grief softens over time; clinical depression does not. With grief, after the numbing and chaotic early days, weeks, and months have passed, your daily schedule begins to proceed as usual. If you are clinically depressed, you may be unable to function day to day.

NORMAL GRIEF	CLINICAL DEPRESSION
You have normal grief if you...	*You may be clinically depressed if you...*
respond to comfort and support.	do not accept support.
are often openly angry.	are irritable and complain but do not directly express anger.
relate your depressed feelings to the loss experience.	do not relate your feelings of depression to a particular life event.
can still experience moments of enjoyment in life.	exhibit an all-pervading sense of doom.
exhibit feelings of sadness and emptiness.	project a sense of hope-lessness and chronic emptiness.
may have transient physical complaints.	have chronic physical complaints.
express guilt over some specific aspect of the loss.	have generalized feelings of guilt.
feel a temporary loss of self-esteem	feel a deep and ongoing loss of self-esteem.

GRIEF AND CLINICAL DEPRESSION AT THE SAME TIME?

Is it possible to be experiencing normal grief *and* clinical depression? The answer is yes.

Depression overlaid on top of grief can take normal and necessary symptoms of grief and make them more severe and debilitating.

Also, clinical depression can make grief last longer than it might otherwise and even worsen. Sometimes clinical depression inhibits your ability to actively mourn.

Also, the normal depression of grief can develop into clinical depression. Regardless of the event (such as a death) or stresses that may initiate a depression, it can persist and progress to the point where its effects continue without relief and independent of what initiated it. At that point the death or other loss may no longer be a potent stressor, but the altered biological processes that manifest themselves as depression have already occurred and can exert their influences on every aspect of your physical, cognitive, emotional, social, and spiritual self.

GRIEF AND THE DSM-5

The DSM, or *Diagnostic and Statistical Manual of Mental Disorders*, is the bible used by counselors and psychiatrists to diagnose and determine how to treat mental health problems. It is published by the American Psychiatric Association.

In the DSM you will find the definitions and symptoms lists for all the types of depression. You will also find a discussion of normal grief following the death of someone loved.

The current edition is called the DSM-5. It was published in May 2013. In earlier DSM versions, depression that followed the death of a loved one excluded someone from being diagnosed with clinical depression after just two weeks' duration of symptoms except in cases of suicidal thoughts, psychosis, or extreme impairment in everyday functioning. Now, under the DSM-5, this so-called "bereavement exclusion" has been removed. What I am calling the normal and necessary depression of grief can now be diagnosed as clinical depression as little as two weeks after a death.

To be fair, the DSM-5 also includes guidelines to help the
clinician distinguish between ordinary grief and major
depression. For example, the manual makes note of the fact
that grieving people are often able to feel a variety of feelings,
including not just sadness but also happier emotions, while
depressed people feel stuck in sadness. Depressed people
feel pain constantly, whereas grieving people experience their
pain in waves. And grieving people have hope for the future,
whereas depressed people feel hopeless.

**These distinctions and others the DSM provides are
helpful, but I am among the many grief counselors who
believe that the DSM-5 is a dangerous step toward
characterizing grief as a medical condition that should be
treated away instead of a normal and necessary spiritual
journey that is healed over the course of months and
years through active and ongoing mourning.**

TYPES OF CLINICAL DEPRESSION

There are several forms of depressive disorders that fall under the
category of clinical depression.

Major depressive disorder, or *major depression,* is characterized
by a combination of symptoms that interfere with a person's ability
to work, sleep, study, eat, and enjoy once-pleasurable activities.
Major depression is disabling and prevents a person from functioning
normally. Some people may experience only a single episode within
their lifetime, but more often a person may have multiple episodes.

Dysthymic disorder, or *dysthymia,* is characterized by long-term
(two years or longer) symptoms that may not be severe enough to
disable a person but can prevent normal functioning or feeling well.

People with dysthymia may also experience one or more episodes of major depression during their lifetimes.

Minor depression is characterized by having symptoms for two weeks or longer that do not meet the full criteria for major depression. Without treatment, people with minor depression are at high risk for developing major depressive disorder.

Anaclitic depression is defined as (and stems from) "the loss of nurturing support systems." As we've said, an important part of mourning is expressing your thoughts and feelings to others and receiving and accepting their support in return. But if you lack adequate support when you experience grief and loss in your life, you are at risk for anaclitic depression. Common symptoms include withdrawal, chronic sadness, and an apparent disinterest in the world around you. It is often very difficult for the person who suffers from this subtype of depression to seek and accept support. These people are often dependent on someone who cares about them to recognize the depression and get them the help they need and deserve.

Masked depression is an area of depression that sometimes gets overlooked. It is associated with what is called *alexithymia*, literally, "without words." This is when the person experiencing moods can't identify them or describe them. This disconnect creates "masked depression," "covert depression," or what I refer to as "converted mourning." This type of depression manifests itself in a variety of behaviors that may seem incompatible with depression, including alcohol abuse and other addictive behaviors such as work, gambling, or sex; anger and aggressive behaviors; accidental injuries; and physical complaints. Overtly avoiding or repressing feelings of grief and loss may lead to indirect behavioral or somatic expressions of the denied emotional experience. We often see masked depression more in men than in women, but it can and does occur in both genders.

There are also other forms of depression with more unique features. However, not everyone agrees on how to characterize and define these forms of depression. They include:

Psychotic depression, which is a combination of severe depression and some form of psychosis, such as having disturbing false beliefs or a break with reality (delusions), or hearing or seeing upsetting things that others cannot hear or see (hallucinations).

Postpartum depression, which is much more serious than the "baby blues" that many women experience after giving birth, when hormonal and physical changes and the new responsibility of caring for a newborn can be overwhelming. It is thought that 10 to 15 percent of women experience this form of depression after giving birth.

A SPECIAL WARNING:

If you were diagnosed with any type of clinical depression before the recent loss in your life, be certain to see a professional caregiver. You will benefit from professional support for your journey. Remember— seeking help is a form of compassionate self-care, not self-indulgence.

Seasonal affective disorder (SAD), which is characterized by the onset of depression during the winter months, when there is less natural sunlight. The depression generally lifts during spring and summer.

Bipolar disorder, which used to be called manic-depression, is not as common as major depression or dysthymia. Bipolar disorder is characterized by cycling mood changes—from extreme highs (i.e., mania) to extreme lows (i.e., depression).

SUICIDE AND DEPRESSION

Transitory thoughts of suicide may occur during your grief journey. Hundreds of grieving people have shared with me thoughts on the order of, "I wouldn't mind if I didn't wake up tomorrow." Comments like this reflect a need to further explore the depth of your sadness.

However—and this is a critically important distinction—it may be normal to experience these passive, passing, and rather vague suicidal thoughts, but it is *not* natural to want, or make plans, to take your own life. Do you see the difference?

If you have been actively thinking of taking your own life, talk to a professional helper immediately. Suicidal thoughts are sometimes an expression of wanting to find relief from the pain of your grief. Yes, you have been injured and you hurt. But to help your injury heal, you must openly express what this loss has meant for you. And you may need professional help as well. If in doubt, seek the support of a professional caregiver immediately.

GOOD GRIEF OR COMPLICATED GRIEF?

Mourning is the normal expression of thoughts and feelings you experience when you lose something or someone of great value to you. As we have emphasized, it is a necessary, although painful, part of your grief journey. By openly embracing your pain, you will, over time and with the support of others, heal from your emotional wounds and reconcile this significant loss in a positive way.

Some counselors refer to this process as "good" grief. And some people find that seeing a counselor to facilitate this good grief process is helpful. A skilled professional can sometimes ease your grief journey and affirm that you are doing the best things you can for you to help yourself heal. I would also note that some lay

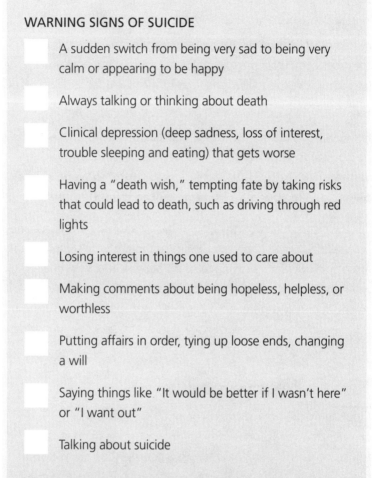

WARNING SIGNS OF SUICIDE

A sudden switch from being very sad to being very calm or appearing to be happy

Always talking or thinking about death

Clinical depression (deep sadness, loss of interest, trouble sleeping and eating) that gets worse

Having a "death wish," tempting fate by taking risks that could lead to death, such as driving through red lights

Losing interest in things one used to care about

Making comments about being hopeless, helpless, or worthless

Putting affairs in order, tying up loose ends, changing a will

Saying things like "It would be better if I wasn't here" or "I want out"

Talking about suicide

If you or someone you care about is exhibiting any of these warning signs, call your local suicide hotline immediately. Call 1-800-SUICIDE (1-800-784-2433) or 1-800-273-TALK (1-800-273-8255) or the deaf hotline at 1-800-799-4TTY (1-800-799-4889). Or go to the nearest emergency room for immediate help.

people (trained or natural caregivers) can also be fantastic "grief companions," as can formal or informal support groups.

Good grief, however, can turn bad. If normal grief strays off course, the work of mourning can go on and on without the grieving person ever reaching reconciliation. It essential to find a trained grief counselor to help you if you are experiencing this "complicated" grief.

"Grief does not change you, Hazel. It reveals you."

— John Green,
The Fault in Our Stars

How can you tell if your grief is complicated? (Of course, keep in mind that grief is naturally complicated!) Any one of these factors could complicate your grief experience:

An unnatural or untimely death. Your grief might be complicated if the person you loved died suddenly or unexpectedly, or if the death was a suicide or a homicide.

Your personality. If you have unreconciled feelings or conflicts relating to other losses in your life ("carried grief"; see pages 63-70), or if you have a tendency toward depression, you may be more susceptible to a complicated grief experience. Difficulties in expressing and integrating feelings of sadness and anger, extreme dependency on the approval of others, or a tendency to assume too much responsibility also may complicate your grief journey.

Your relationship with the person who died. An intensely close relationship to the person who died (especially if you lack other support systems) may trigger complicated grieving, as might unreconciled conflicts or a history of abuse with that person.

An inability to express your grief. If you have been unable to accept the intense emotions evoked by the death, you may experience complicated grief. Or perhaps your family and friends have failed to validate your feelings of loss. Other significant losses occurring at the same time, the inability to participate in the grief process due to personal illness, or the lack of access to the usual rituals, such as a funeral, also may provide the impetus for complicated grief.

Use of drugs or alcohol. Drugs or alcohol may suppress your feelings connected with the loss, thus short-circuiting what may otherwise be a normal and healthy grief journey.

> *"Everyone grieves in different ways. For some, it could take longer or shorter. I do know it never disappears. An ember still smolders inside me. Most days, I don't notice it, but, out of the blue, it'll flare to life."*
>
> — Maria V. Snyder

In my work as a grief counselor, I am often faced with the need to untangle the subtle differences of forms of "complicated grief." I only use this framework to assist me in creating a plan of action to be of the most help I possibly can. Below I outline the framework I use at my Center for Loss and Life Transition. Keep in mind these symptoms are not always neatly defined or mutually exclusive:

1. **Absent or delayed grief**

   Absent or delayed grief seems to be nonexistent. When someone experiences a loss but is not given the opportunity (or does not perceive a need) to mourn, grief may seem to be absent but is only, in fact, delayed or "carried." (See pages 63-70.) This happens to some people in their childhood and teenage years if they are "forgotten mourners." Of course, after a significant loss, denial is normal and necessary for a short time, during those early days of shock and numbness, but ongoing denial or postponement is harmful and a sign of complicated grief.

2. Distorted grief

Distorted grief is grief that seems to focus on one particular thought or feeling. Instead of the symptoms softening, it hardens and gets locked in place—thus it is distorted and covers up underlying emotions like hurt, pain, fear, and helplessness. If someone who has experienced a significant loss is extremely angry all the time, to the exclusion of other grief dimensions, for example, I would suspect complicated grief. I also often see distorted grief expressing itself as guilt (where the person self-punishes), anxiety (where panic attacks set in), and, the topic of this book, depression (where the normal and necessary sadness of grief becomes clinical depression).

3. Converted grief

Converted grief can have a number of appearances.

One is grief in which the intense feelings of loss are displaced, or directed at other situations or people. For example, some grievers with converted grief begin to have trouble at work or in relationships with other people. They may feel depressed,

> *"Grief is like sinking, like being buried. I am in water the tawny color of kicked-up dirt. Every breath is full of choking. There is nothing to hold on to, no sides, no way to claw myself up. There is nothing to do but let go.*
>
> *"Let go. Feel the weight all around you, feel the squeezing of your lungs, the slow, low pressure. Let yourself go deeper. There is nothing but bottom. There is nothing but the taste of metal, and the echoes of old things, and days that look like darkness."*
>
> — Lauren Oliver

bitter, and hateful, yet unaware that those feelings are, in actuality, tied to their loss.

Other times converted grief is replaced. If the griever takes the emotions that were invested in the relationship that ended in death and reinvests them prematurely in another relationship, he may be attempting to replace his grief. This replacement pattern does not only occur with other relationships, but in other life activities as well. For example, he may become a workaholic although he has never been one in the past.

Sometimes converters minimize or intellectualize their grief. If they are aware of their feelings of grief but try to downplay them, or if they try to prove to themselves that the loss doesn't affect them very much, they may be minimizing their grief. Or they may talk openly about how "well they are doing" and how "their life is back to normal," even though the loss is recent.

Finally, some converters somaticize their grief. Somaticizing is the clinical term for converting emotions into physical symptoms. You may become so completely preoccupied with your physical problems that you have little or no energy to relate to other people or do your work of mourning.

Other converters exchange their grief for addictive behaviors. Many abuse drugs or alcohol, but others become addicted to exercise, shopping, sex, gambling, or other repetitive physical actions. Any form of addictive behavior in response to loss merits the assistance of a skilled and compassionate grief counselor.

4. Chronic grief

Chronic grief is when you experience acute symptoms of grief (inability to experience pleasure, confusion, difficulty focusing, and lethargy) that do not change or soften over time. Consciously or unconsciously, you may be attempting to keep the dead person alive. Warning: Many people who don't know much about grief label people as "chronic" mourners. So be careful with any of these labels that I mention here in an effort to aid in your understanding. Remember, you are doing the best you know how to do even if you are struggling.

Instead of "complicated grief," the DSM uses the term "Persistent Complex Bereavement Disorder" to describe (in very clinical terms and with very precise diagnostic criteria) intense grief that continues to prevent a person from functioning a year or more after the death.

No matter what you call it, complicated grief is grief that has somehow been pulled off the path and needs to find its way back to it. Depression may or may not be part of complicated grief and may or may not be the cause of complicated grief.

HOW TO KNOW IF YOU ARE CLINICALLY DEPRESSED OR EXPERIENCING COMPLICATED GRIEF

In this chapter I have presented the distinguishing features of clinical depression and symptoms of complicated grief. I have also suggested some differences between "good grief" and clinical depression or complicated grief.

But in truth, **the boundaries around each of these categories are blurry and somewhat arbitrary**. The bottom line is that if after reading this chapter you think you might be struggling with clinical depression or complicated grief, I urge you to seek the help of a professional therapist. Even for people in the throes of "good grief," a sensitive grief counselor will be your ally and advocate.

Ultimately, what matters is not the label that is placed on your grief and depression but rather receiving the help and support you need.

And remember—deciding to seek professional help from a counselor or therapist is not an admission of failure; it is a positive step in your personal development and an important self-care task.

WHAT TO DO ABOUT DEPRESSION

Here is the good news: Whether you are experiencing the normal and necessary depression of grief, complicated grief, or clinical depression (or grief *and* depression!), help is available. With appropriate assessment and treatment, most people with depression will find relief.

> *"Depression is the inability to construct a future."*
>
> — Rollo May

If you even suspect you are clinically depressed, it is critically important that you take steps to get help. Untreated depression can raise your risk for a number of additional health problems, including insomnia, overweight, heart disease, high blood pressure, and recurring or deeper depression. It may well also prevent you from moving forward in your journey through grief.

In the next chapter we'll look at what I consider the gold standard "treatment" for normal, uncomplicated grief (and why I normally never use the term "treatment"!).

PART 4:

Mourning as "treatment"

You are probably reading this book because on the inside you are experiencing some or all of the symptoms of grief we explored in Part 1 of this resource. You may in particular be struggling with sadness. And you might also be mired in clinical depression.

So that is the stew of thoughts, feelings, and symptoms roiling around inside you. Basically, you feel lousy and in despair. But what can you do about it?

You can mourn. Remember how in Part 1 we defined mourning as the outward expression of grief? Mourning is expressing all of your symptoms outside of yourself. Mourning is how you heal.

Mourning is treatment, if you will. If you have clinical depression, you may also need medical treatment, but if your depression is in part

> "*Depression can kill you. It can also be a spiritually enriching experience. It's really an important part of my theology now and my spirituality that life is not perfect, and I grew up wanting it to be and thinking that if it wasn't, I could make it that way, and I had to acknowledge that I had all kinds of flaws and sadnesses and problems.*"
>
> — Krista Tippett

caused by loss, there is no getting around the fact that mourning is an essential component of your journey back to well-being.

I'd like to point out here that I don't usually like to use the word "treatment" when it comes to grief. The term implies that grief is a disease that must be cured. But grief is definitely not a disease. It is the normal and natural aftermath of losing someone or something that you love.

> *"My feet will want to walk to where you are sleeping, but I shall go on living."*
>
> — Pablo Neruda

But because depression can also be a very real medical condition, **I am using the term treatment here to emphasize that no matter what, mourning is essential**. It is always the right thing to do when you are grieving. If you have clinical depression, your treatment may also include antidepressants or other medical options (discussed in the next chapter), but mourning will still be central to your eventual healing.

THE SIX NEEDS OF MOURNING

Although each person's grief journey is unique, all grievers share six central needs of mourning. These are the needs they must meet, the "yield signs" on the journey, the challenges that grief sets before them.

Although they are numbered one through six, the six needs of mourning are not orderly or predictable. You will probably jump around in random fashion while working on them, and at any given time you will probably be working on more than one at once. You will address each need when you are ready to do so.

It is important for you to understand that these needs are not about trying to get you to "move on with life." Rather, they are about the need to dose yourself with grief as you authentically mourn. In other words, they are not a checklist. Instead, they are touchstones on your spiritual journey.

Your awareness of these needs, however, will give you a participatory, action-oriented approach to healing in grief as opposed to a perception of grief as something you passively experience.

And to cope with and ultimately transcend your depression, actively expressing your grief is the way.

THE SIX NEEDS OF MOURNING

1. Accept the reality of the death.

2. Let yourself feel the pain of the loss.

3. Remember the person who died.

4. Develop a new self-identity.

5. Search for meaning.

6. Let others help you—now and always.

Mourning Need 1:
Accept the reality of the death

You can know something in your head but not in your heart. This is what often happens when you experience a significant loss. This first need of mourning involves gently confronting the reality of the loss even as you learn how to have a new form of relationship with the person who died (see mourning need 3).

If someone you love has died, this need involves accepting the reality that this person will never physically come back into your life again. To survive, you may try to push away the reality of the death at times. But to acknowledge that someone you love has died is a process, not an event; embracing this painful reality is not quick, easy, or efficient.

You may move back and forth between protesting and encountering the reality of the death. You may discover yourself replaying events surrounding the death and confronting memories, both good and bad.

Talk with someone who will listen without judging about your normal and necessary struggle to accept the reality. Talk through the events surrounding the death that you keep thinking about and the memories that you keep remembering.

Ruminating is known to be a major component of depression. Ruminating means dwelling on and brooding over painful thoughts and scenarios. In grief, it's normal and necessary to replay events and thoughts in your mind. It's how your brain and eventually your heart come to terms with a reality that's hard to understand. But I agree that ruminating on the inside *without also expressing those thoughts and scenarios on the outside* stalls this need of mourning and will only further compound your depression.

> "To live into the future depends on my response to the reality of what I am experiencing. Temporarily, I need to create insulation from the full force of what I am coming to know. If I felt it all at once, I might die. But feel it I must."
>
> — A. Wolfelt

> "There is a sacredness in tears. They are not the mark of weakness but of power. They speak more eloquently than ten thousand tongues. They are messengers of overwhelming grief... and unspeakable love."
>
> — Washington Irving

Remember, the idea here is to take whatever's going on inside and express it. Your mind may be revisiting this need over and over, but to mourn it, you must get it outside your mind. Talking, journaling, writing letters, blogging, vlogging, making art—these are all ways to work on this important need.

Mourning Need 2: Let yourself feel the pain of the loss

This need of mourning requires us to embrace the pain of our loss—something we naturally don't want to do. It is easier to avoid, repress, or deny the pain of grief than it is to confront it, yet it is in confronting our pain—or, as we have said, making friends with it—that we learn to reconcile ourselves to it.

Yet if you are reading this book, you are probably already feeling your sadness. You may have tried to avoid, repress, or deny it, but it wouldn't let you. The good news is that in feeling your pain, you are on the right path. Now you must begin to work on expressing that pain.

Find others with whom you can share your painful thoughts and feelings; friends who listen without judging are your most important helpers as you work on this mourning need. Support groups, where people come together and share the common bond of experience, can be invaluable in supporting your need to express your pain. In the safety of a support group, you will be allowed and gently encouraged to talk about your thoughts and feelings as much and as often as you like. Participating in online grief forums is another way to mourn, but only if you are contributing and not merely lurking.

> "I may try to protect myself from my sadness by not talking about my loss. I may even secretly hope that the person who died will come back if I don't talk about it. Yet, as difficult as it is, I must feel it to heal it."
>
> — A. Wolfelt

Other ways of mourning your pain include writing poetry, journaling, writing letters to the person who died, praying, singing along to sad songs, and making paintings or collages that depict your feelings.

Never forget that grief is a process, not an event. Your pain will probably ebb and flow for months, even years; embracing it when it washes over you will require patience, support, and strength.

You will probably discover that you need to dose yourself in embracing your pain. In other words, you cannot (nor should you try to) overload yourself with the hurt all at one time. Sometimes you may need to distract yourself from the pain of the death, while at other times you will need to create a safe place to move toward it.

Feeling your pain can sometimes zap you of your energy. When your energy is low, you may be tempted to suppress your grief or even run from it. If you start running and keep running, you may never heal. Dose your pain: yes! Deny your pain: no!

Unfortunately, as I have said, our culture tends to encourage the denial of pain. We misunderstand the role of suffering. If you openly express your feelings of grief, misinformed friends may advise you to "carry on" or "keep your chin up." If, on the other hand, you remain "strong" and "in control," you may be congratulated for "doing well" with your grief. Actually, doing well with your grief means becoming well acquainted with your pain. Don't let others deny you this critical mourning need.

As you encounter your pain, you will also need to nurture yourself physically, cognitively, emotionally, socially, and spiritually. Eat well, rest often, and exercise regularly.

Mourning Need 3: Remember the person who died

Do you have any kind of relationship with people after they die?
Of course. You have a relationship of memory. Precious memories,
dreams reflecting the significance of the relationship, and objects
that link you to the person who died (such as photos, souvenirs,
clothing, etc.) are examples of
some of the things that give
testimony to a different form of a
continued relationship. This need
of mourning involves allowing and
encouraging yourself to pursue this
relationship. As Morrie Schwartz
noted, "Death ends a life, not a
relationship."

Embracing your memories can be
a very slow and, at times, painful
process. In fact, you may want
to avoid your memories because
they are only making you sadder.
You may even be drinking, taking
drugs, or "keeping busy" in

> *"The essence of finding
> meaning in the future
> is not to forget the past,
> as I have been told, but
> instead to embrace my
> past. For it is in listening
> to the music of the past
> that I can sing in the pres-
> ent and dance into the
> future."*
>
> — A. Wolfelt

an effort to not remember. But avoidance and denial don't work
forever. What you try to avoid now will only come up later and cause
problems such as anxiety and relationship issues along the way. You
must remember, but in doses. Don't try to do all of your work of
mourning at once. Go slowly and be patient with yourself.

If you are struggling with depression, you may be ruminating about
memories. In other words, you may be replaying a memory or set
of memories over and over in your mind and despairing at the loss
or perhaps regret that these memories makes you feel. Again, with
rumination and depression, the key is to express those memories

outside of yourself. Talk to someone about them. Write them down and share what you write with someone who cares about you.

In other words, try to be active with your memories. "Do" something with them. Here are some ideas:

• Talk or write out your favorite memories.

• Give yourself permission to keep some special keepsakes or "linking objects"

• Display photos of the person who died.

• Visit places of special significance that stimulate memories of times shared together.

• Review photo albums at special times such as holidays, birthdays, and anniversaries.

Perhaps one of the best ways to embrace memories is through creating a "Memory Book" that contains special photographs you have selected and perhaps other memorabilia such as ticket stubs, menus, etc. Organize these items, place them in an album, and write out the memories reflected in the photos. Will you feel sad while you are working on this memory book? Yes, but what I have learned is that people feel more sadness and despair when they are ruminating about memories than when they are doing something with those memories. It's as if the act of expression and creation begins to transform the despair into hope.

> "Start by doing what's necessary; then do what's possible; and suddenly you are doing the impossible."
>
> — St. Francis of Assisi

I also need to mention here the reality that memories are not always pleasant. If you have memories of violence, abuse, trauma, angry outbursts, or other such moments, addressing this need of mourning can be even more difficult. To ignore painful or ambivalent memories is to prevent yourself from healing. You will need someone who can non-judgmentally explore any difficult memories with you. If you repress or deny these memories, you risk carrying an underlying sadness or anger into your future.

> *"Memories are the key not to the past, but to the future."*
>
> — Corrie Ten Boom

In my experience, remembering the past makes hoping for the future possible. Your future will become open to new experiences only to the extent that you embrace the past.

Mourning Need 4: Develop a new self-identity

Your personal identity, or self-perception, is the result of the ongoing process of establishing a sense of who you are. Part of your self-identity comes from the relationships you have with other people. When someone with whom you have a relationship dies, your self-identity, or the way you see yourself, naturally changes.

You may have gone from being a "wife" or "husband" to a "widow" or "widower." You may have gone from being a "parent" to a "bereaved parent." The way you define yourself and the way

> *"Now I realize: I knew myself so little. This death has forced me to become reacquainted with myself. I must slow down and listen."*
>
> — A. Wolfelt

society defines you is changed. This facet of grief can feel very
wounding because not only has a unique person you were attached
to been taken away, but part of the you that is left behind is now
also changed. And usually this change is not something you would
choose for yourself.

What's more, a death often requires you to take on new roles that
had been filled by the person who died. After all, someone still
has to take out the garbage, buy the groceries, and balance the
checkbook. You confront your changed identity every time you do
something that used to be done by the person who died. This can
be very hard work and, at
times, can leave you feeling
very drained of emotional,
physical, and spiritual
energy, compounding your
depression.

> *"Not until we are lost do
> we begin to understand
> ourselves."*
>
> — Henry David Thoreau

Developing a new self-identity
is painful but necessary—just
like all the other needs of mourning. Do what you need to do in order
to survive, at least for now, as you try to re-anchor yourself. To be
dependent on others as you struggle with a changed identity does not
make you weak, bad, or inferior. Your self-identity has been assaulted.
Be compassionate with yourself. Accept the support of others.

Reaching out to others is a form of mourning, of course. Sharing
your self-identity thoughts and feelings in the safety of a support
group is another. Talking to a counselor is a third. Find a way to
express your struggles with, and pain over, being forced to develop a
new self-identity.

As you address this need, be certain to keep other major changes to
a minimum if at all possible. Now is not the time for a major move or

addition to the house. Your energy is already depleted. Don't deplete it even more by making significant changes or taking on too many tasks.

Mourning Need 5: Search for meaning

When someone you love dies, you naturally question the meaning and purpose of life. You probably will question your philosophy of life and explore religious and spiritual values as you work on this need. You may discover yourself searching for meaning in your continued living as you ask "How?" and "Why?" questions. "How could God let this happen?" "Why did this happen now, in this way?" The death reminds you of your lack of control. It can leave you feeling powerless.

The person who died was a part of you. This death means you mourn a loss not only outside of yourself, but inside of yourself as well. At times, overwhelming sadness and loneliness may be your constant companions. You may feel that when this person died, part of you died with him or her. And now you are faced with finding some meaning in going on with your life even though you may often feel so empty.

Searching for meaning is a mourning need, which means that it's a task your soul requires. But it's a hard task, and a painful one. And to top it off, there are no easy or firm answers to the "How?" and "Why?" questions. Which means you can spend many

> *"I must encounter my questions, my doubts, my fears. There is richness in these domains. As I explore them, I don't reinforce my tensions but instead release them. In this way I transcend my grief and discover new life beyond anything my heart could ever have comprehended. Oh the gentleness of new life."*
>
> — A. Wolfelt

long, difficult hours searching for an answer you don't ever find.

The despair and hopelessness of grief stem, in large part, from the search for meaning. The challenge of the human condition is that we are aware of our own mortality and the mortality of those we love, yet many of us feel uncertain about what happens after death. So we struggle to find understanding and assurances that life is worth living and all will be well.

> "During depression the world disap-pears ... because the inner voice is so urgent in its own discourse: How shall I live? How shall I man-age the future? Why should I go on?"
>
> — Kate Millett

That struggle is at the heart of the depression of grief. As we have said, grief is first and foremost a spiritual journey. And the search for meaning is a spiritual search. This death calls for you to confront your own spirituality. You may doubt your faith and have spiritual conflicts and questions racing through your head and heart. This is normal and part of your journey toward renewed living. You might feel distant from your God or Higher Power, even questioning the very existence of God. You may rage at your God. Such feelings of doubt are normal.

As with the other mourning needs, the way to mourn this aspect of your grief is to share it. Talk to others about your struggle to find meaning—especially others whose faith or spirituality you admire. Join a support group at a church, temple, or mosque. Beware of the religious person who preaches that doubt and questioning are sinful or wrong, however. God can handle your doubts, I always say.

Pray. Try praying out loud. Saying the words that your heart and soul yearn to release gives voice to your grief and can ease your sadness.

Moving your body is also a form of mourning. Walk a prayer labyrinth, hike to a temple on a hill, finger a rosary, or stand up and sing a hymn. All of these forms of movement will help you express your grief.

> "Whatever things are true, whatever things are noble, whatever things are just, whatever things are pure, whatever things are lovely, whatever things are of good report, if there is any virtue and if there is anything praiseworthy—meditate on these things."
>
> — Philippians 4:8
> (New King James Version)

Spending time in "thin places" will as well. In the Celtic tradition, thin places are spots where the separation between the physical world and the spiritual world seem tenuous. They are places where the veil between Heaven and earth, between the holy and the everyday, are so thin that when we are near them, we intuitively sense the timeless, boundless spiritual world. Thin places are usually outdoors, often where water and land meet or land and sky come together. You might find thin places on a riverbank, a beach, or a mountaintop. Go to a thin place to pray, to walk, or to simply sit in the presence of the holy.

Remember—mourners often find themselves questioning their faith for months before they rediscover meaning in life. But be assured: It can be done, even when you don't have all the answers.

Move at your own pace as you recognize that allowing yourself to hurt and finding meaning are not mutually exclusive. More often, your need to mourn and find meaning in your continued living will blend into each other, with the former giving way to the latter as healing occurs.

Mourning Need 6: Let others help you—now and always

The quality and quantity of understanding support you get during
your work of mourning will have a major influence on your capacity
to heal. You cannot—nor should you
try to—do this alone. Drawing on the
experiences and encouragement of
friends, fellow grievers, or professional
counselors is not a weakness but a
healthy human need. And because
mourning is a process that takes
place over time, this support must be
available months and even years after
the death of someone in your life.

> "I heal, in part, by
> allowing others to
> express their love
> for me. By choos-
> ing to invite others
> into my journey,
> I move toward
> health and heal-
> ing. If I hide from
> others, I hide from
> healing."
>
> — A. Wolfelt

Unfortunately, because our society
places so much value on the ability to
"carry on," "keep your chin up," and
"keep busy," many bereaved people
are abandoned shortly after the event
of the death. "It's best not to talk
about the death," "It's over and done
with," and "It's time to get on with
your life" are the types of messages directed at grieving people that
still dominate.

Obviously, these messages encourage you to deny or repress your
grief rather than express it. If you know people who consider
themselves supportive yet offer you these kinds of mourning-
avoiding messages, you'll need to look to others for truly helpful
support. People who see your mourning as something that should
be "overcome" instead of experienced will not help you heal.

To be truly helpful, the people in your support system must
appreciate the impact this death has had on you. They must

understand that in order to heal, you must be allowed—even encouraged—to mourn long after the death. And they must encourage you to see mourning not as an enemy to be vanquished but as a necessity to be experienced as a result of having loved.

Your depression may also be a roadblock to getting this need met, however. When you are depressed, you withdraw. You may lack the energy to leave your house and interact. You may feel worthless and undeserving of the support of others. You may be sitting in your wound, as I have advised is necessary, but you may be doing it so much and for so long that you are cutting yourself off from everyone who cares about you.

If you are not receiving support from others because you have withdrawn, find one friend who can be your lifeline. Tell this friend that you know you need

> *"I am because we are."*
> — African proverb

to be around other people but you also need his help to make this happen. Make an agreement with this friend that when he offers to spend time with you, you will say yes. One compassionate friend with a set of good listening ears and a nonjudgmental heart can make all the difference.

Support groups, where people come together and share the common bond of experience, can be invaluable in helping you and your grief and supporting your need to mourn long after the event of the death. Remind yourself that you deserve and need to have understanding people around you who allow you to feel your grief long after society deems appropriate.

WHAT HAPPENS WHEN YOU DON'T MOURN

When you actively mourn, there is movement. In other words, mourning puts your emotions in motion. As I have said, I use the term "perturbation" to refer to this capacity to experience change and movement. To integrate grief, you must be touched by what you experience *and* you must express what you experience. If you do not allow yourself to be touched, on the other hand, and/or if you do not express what is touching you on the inside, you can't be changed by it. Instead, you may well become "stuck."

> "Pain insists upon being attended to. God whispers to us in our pleasures, speaks in our consciences, but shouts in our pains. It is his megaphone to rouse a deaf world."
>
> — C.S. Lewis

So, if you are grieving but not mourning, you are doing what I call "carrying" your grief. That is, you are carrying it inside you, and you will continue to carry it until you express it.

When you carry your pain instead of mourning it, it will come back to haunt you. It will keep trying to get your attention until you give it the attention it demands and deserves. As Michel de Montaigne once observed, "The man who fears suffering is already suffering from what he fears."

If your pain is left unhealed, it destroys your enthusiasm for life and living. It can deny you your creativity, your gifts, and your talents. The result is that these parts of yourself go stagnant or unclaimed inside of you, wishing they could get out but feeling trapped.

Also keep in mind that carried grief compounds. The sadness and depression you are experiencing today may be the result of not only your most recent loss, but all the unmourned losses from earlier in your life. My experience as a grief counselor and educator tells me that carried grief is often a significant contributor to depression.

Following are some of the common fall-out symptoms I have
observed in people who carry the pains of grief and have not had
the opportunity to authentically mourn. Depression is among them,
but so are other symptoms you may
be experiencing.

Difficulties with trust and intimacy

Many grief-carriers have taught me
that they feel they are unlovable.
Often, this becomes a self-fulfilling
prophecy. You may be aware of the
need for love but at the same time
feel unworthy of it. Feelings of being
unloved can then translate into "I
am unlovable." The tragic result is
often isolation and loneliness. Some
of these people do get married or
attempt to have close relationships
but still keep their distance in an effort
to stay safe.

Grief-carriers often feel, consciously
or subconsciously, that others
will leave them. If you have been
abandoned in your need to mourn
by significant people in your life, you
naturally feel others will also abandon

**POTENTIAL
SYMPTOMS OF
CARRIED GRIEF**

- Difficulties with trust
  and intimacy

- Depression and
  negative outlook

- Anxiety and panic
  attacks

- Psychic numbing and
  disconnection

- Irritability and
  agitation

- Substance abuse,
  addictions, eating
  disorders

- Physical problems,
  real or imagined

you. If you have tried to trust in the past and people betrayed the
trust, you come to believe no one is trustworthy. You don't open
your heart easily, and when you do, you fear others will misuse you
and ultimately go away. So, it becomes safer to stay distant and
closed off.

Sadness and depression

Grief-carriers experience an ongoing loss of their divine spark—
that which gives purpose and meaning to our living. When the
spirit is muted, there is an unending
hampering of the capacity to live life
with meaning and purpose. The result
is often depression and a negative,
cynical view of life.

> *"Depression is*
> *nourished by*
> *a lifetime of*
> *ungrieved and*
> *unforgiven hurts."*
>
> — Penelope Sweet

Depression sometimes reveals itself
as a generally negative outlook on
life. While some grief-carriers don't
experience deep, dark depression,
they suffer from a chronic, low-grade
depression; the world begins to look
gray. They lose their full range of emotional functioning, defending
against ever being really happy or really sad. Sometimes they
rationalize this mood state as "this is just what life is like."

Similarly, feelings of meaninglessness often pervade the lives
of grief-carriers. People who grieve but don't mourn often feel
isolated emotionally and lack a sense of meaning and purpose. They
experience a sense of soullessness or a loss of vitality and enthusiasm
for life and living. They feel empty and alone.

Anxiety and panic attacks

Some grief-carriers struggle with a persistent and generalized
anxiety. Anxiety is often reflected in motor tension (fatigue, muscle
aches, easy startle response); autonomic hyperactivity (dry mouth,
gastrointestinal distress, heart racing); apprehensive expectations
(fears of injury or death); and hyper-vigilance and scanning (hyper-
alertness, irritability, and problems with sleep disturbance). Again,
just as with depression, there can be multiple causes of anxiety;

however, I am certain that carried pain is a contributor for many people.

Anxiety sometimes shows up in the form of panic attacks. Panic is a sudden, overpowering fright. On occasion, these attacks may last for hours, though attacks are typically for a period of minutes, during which the person literally experiences terror. Panic attacks are often recurrent and episodic, though for some people they become chronic.

The human spirit must be connected to others and surrounded in unconditional love. I have seen numerous people in counseling whose panic attacks were the doorway to get them to give attention to carried grief and learn to authentically mourn.

Psychic numbing and disconnection

While shock and numbness are normal early responses in the face of loss, some grief-carriers get so detached that they literally feel disconnected from the world around them. If this is happening to you, you may notice that you can see and hear others around you, but you can't feel them.

> "I learned to be with myself rather than avoiding myself with limiting habits; I started to be aware of my feelings more, rather than numb them."
>
> — Judith Wright

The result is that the world and the people in it seem unreal. You may live your days feeling you are in a daze, going through the motions yet not feeling present to others and even yourself. Some people describe this as a dream-like state with feelings of unreality. You are existing but not really alive to what is going on around you.

Numbing results in a feeling of existing but not really living. The
muting power of numbness prevents you from experiencing any of
the positive things that may be going on around you. You are literally
disconnected from the world and yourself.

Irritability and agitation

Some grief-carriers express their pain indirectly through irritability
and agitation. These symptoms may show up at work, at home, or
anywhere they can find expression. It is like you are in a pressure
cooker, and you are trying to release the pressure. In its extreme
form, this symptom may show up as uncontrolled anger or rage.

These emotions of protest are often an unconscious attempt to fight
off the underlying, more primary emotions of pain, helplessness,
hurt, isolation, and aloneness. People around you who sense or
experience your irritability and agitation avoid you, resulting in more
carried pain and less authentic mourning.

Substance abuse, addictions, eating disorders

Many grief-carriers will self-treat their pain through substance
abuse, addictive behaviors, and eating disorders. Modern society
provides an increasing number of
substances that might be abused. People
are usually abusive of or addicted to
a specific substance such as alcohol,
cocaine, or food. However, grief-carriers
can also be addicted to activities, such as
destructive relationships, sex, smoking,
gambling, work, exercise, achievement,
over-caretaking of others, religiosity, and
materialism. These substances and activities are ways the person tries
to move away from or deny the pain of life losses.

> "In the middle
> of difficulty lies
> opportunity."
>
> — Albert Einstein

Addictions serve to numb the grief-carrier's feelings, sapping your spirit or "life force," and locking you into living a life that feels muted and lacking in purpose and positive direction. Self-treating carried pain through addictions prevents you from deeper satisfactions and any kind of spiritual fulfillment. And unfortunately, many addictions result in a slow but steady process of self-destruction.

Physical problems, real or imagined

If we don't mourn one way, it comes out another. Many grief-carriers store the pain in their bodies. The result is that the immune system breaks down and illness surfaces.

When people shut down, deny, or inhibit mourning, they sometimes assume a "sick role" in an effort to legitimize not feeling well to those around them. They "somaticize" their feelings of grief, which means they unconsciously turn their emotional and spiritual hurts into physical ones. This often results in frequent visits to the physician's office. Sometimes the physical symptoms are very real; other times they are imagined. These imagined symptoms are like a silent voice crying out for the need to give expression to the carried pain. Typically, there are no organic findings to support a physical diagnosis.

We should note that somaticizing is different than the person who experiences real physical illness after a loss. Many formal studies have documented significant increases in illness following the experience of a variety of losses in life, particularly death loss. However, somaticizing grief as the chief mechanism of mourning is a means of avoiding grief. You may truly feel sick, but medically speaking there is not anything really wrong with you. Quite simply, life cannot re-inhabit the body until we mourn our life losses. The result is that you can feel sick, if not dead, while you are alive. The good news is that carried griefs stored in the body can be integrated into life as long as their causes are not denied. As you begin to embrace the emotional and spiritual pain, the bodily pain eases.

CARRIED GRIEF SELF-INVENTORY

Now that you've explored some of the common symptoms of carried grief, I'd like you to consider the possible sources of any pain you might carry. The purpose of inventorying your losses and acknowledging these potential symptoms is not to discourage or shame you, but to ultimately empower you.

> *"One heals suffering only by experiencing it to the full."*
>
> — Marcel Proust

The following Loss Inventory lists many types of losses commonly suffered by humankind. I invite you to skim the list and circle or put a checkmark next to the types of losses that you have experienced. This list is not comprehensive, of course, so I'd also like you to use the blank lines on page 72 to write down all the significant losses in your life, including those that may not be listed here.

Loss of people you love

  Separation (physical and/or emotional)

  Rejection

  Hostility/grudges

  Illness (such as Alzheimer's, debilitating conditions)

  Divorce

  Abandonment/betrayal

  Death

  Empty nest

Loss of pets

Loss of aspects of self

- Self-esteem (often through physical, sexual, or emotional abuse or rape, humiliation, rejection, or neglect)
- Health, physical, or mental ability
- Job (downsizing, firing, failed business, retirement)
- Control (such as through addiction, victimization)
- Innocence (such as through abuse, exposure to immoral behavior)
- Sexual identity/ability/desire
- Security (such as through financial problems, war)
- Expectations about how our lives should/would be
- Reputation
- Beliefs (religious, spiritual, belief in others we trusted)
- Dreams (cherished hopes for the future)

Loss of physical objects

- Home (such as through a physical disaster, move, or transition into assisted living environments)
- Linking objects (special items such as photos that carry emotional weight)
- Money
- Belongings (through theft or fire, etc.)
- Nature/place (through a move, changing land use)

Loss through developmental transitions

- Toddlerhood to childhood
- Childhood to adolescence
- Adolescence to adulthood
- Leaving home
- Marriage
- Having/not having children
- Mid-life
- Taking care of parents
- Retirement
- Old age

My personal loss inventory:

_____

_____

_____

_____

_____

_____

After you've completed your personal loss inventory, go back and circle or highlight those losses that you think may be contributing to any pain you might be carrying. How do you know which are most significant for you? As you're perusing your list, pause for a moment on each item and note which elicit the most emotion. Which make you feel the most sad? The most angry? The most fear? The most pain? Whether they seem significant on the surface or not, these are likely your deepest sources of carried grief. For example, having been fired from a job may, for you, have resulted in more carried pain than the death of a family member, especially if you mourned the death but not the job loss.

Now that you've inventoried the types of losses you've experienced in your life, I encourage you to answer the following questions.

Circle the word that most applies to how you authentically feel.

1. Do you have difficulties with trust and intimacy?

   Never   Seldom   Occasionally   Often   Usually

2. Do you have a tendency toward depression
   and a negative outlook?

   Never   Seldom   Occasionally   Often   Usually

3. Do you have difficulties with anxiety and/or panic attacks?

   Never   Seldom   Occasionally   Often   Usually

4. Do you have trouble with psychic numbing and disconnection?

   Never   Seldom   Occasionally   Often   Usually

5. Do you have difficulties with irritability and agitation?

   Never   Seldom   Occasionally   Often   Usually

6. Do you struggle with substance abuse, addictions, or eating
   disorders?

   Never   Seldom   Occasionally   Often   Usually

7. Do you have any physical problems, real or imagined?

   Never   Seldom   Occasionally   Often   Usually

8. Do you find it easier to take care of others than you do to care for yourself?

Never	Seldom	Occasionally	Often	Usually

9. Do you find it difficult to express your feelings?

Never	Seldom	Occasionally	Often	Usually

10. Do you find it difficult to ask for what you want from other people?

Never	Seldom	Occasionally	Often	Usually

11. Do you feel a lack of meaning and purpose in your life?

Never	Seldom	Occasionally	Often	Usually

If you answered "Occasionally," "Often," or "Usually" to any of these questions, you may well be carrying grief from earlier losses in your life in addition to your most recent loss. Acknowledging and authentically mourning your grief will take time, commitment, and discipline. But, the good news is that you must want to do it or you wouldn't be reading this book. Your life exactly as it is contains just what is needed for your own journey of healing the carried pain of grief.

THE POWER OF TELLING YOUR STORY

Love is never the same twice and neither is grief. Each is a one-of-a-kind story, a snowflake in the history of humanity. Part of your grief work now is to tell your story, even as it continues to unfold and morph into something ever new.

In fact, after someone you love dies, the creation of renewed meaning and purpose in your life requires that you "re-story" your life. As you know, your grief experience is unique and personal.

Although even the most compassionate person cannot completely comprehend what this is like for you, you will find comfort and support when you surround yourself with people who will honor your story of love and loss.

The thoughts and feelings that bubble up when someone loved dies often feel heavy and overpowering. Expressing what this experience is like for you—telling the story of your love and your grief—is one way to release the pain that has permeated your heart. Expressing yourself can bring some light into the midst of the dark because it will allow you to feel heard, understood, and loved.

Find people who make you feel safe and will truly listen—who will let you share without trying to fix, take way, or distract you from what you are feeling. If telling your story is difficult for you, take time to write it out and then share it with someone. Consider drawing or making something that represents what your grief journey feels like. Perhaps you can communicate your story through art instead of words with someone who is able to simply take in what you are communicating. Share your story in whatever way feels natural to you.

> *"There is no greater agony than bearing an untold story inside you."*
>
> — Maya Angelou

Because stories of love and loss take time, patience, and unconditional love, they serve as powerful antidotes to a modern society that is all too often preoccupied with getting you to "let go," "move on," and "find closure." Whether you share your story with a friend, a family member, a coworker, or a fellow traveler in grief whom you've met through a support group, having others bear witness to the telling of your unique story is one way to go backward on the pathway to eventually going forward.

Honoring your one-of-a-kind story invites you to slow down, turn inward, and create the sacred space to do so. Having a place to have your story honored allows you to embrace what needs to be embraced and come to understand that you can and will come out of the dark and into the light.

You heal yourself as you tell the tale. This is the awesome power of story.

PART 5:

Medical therapies as treatment

So far in this book we have said that it is normal, natural, and necessary to be depressed when you are grieving. Befriending, expressing, and working through your sorrow, in fact, is how you heal your wound and prepare yourself to go on to live and love fully again.

> "The human body experiences a powerful gravitational pull in the direction of hope. That is why the patient's hopes are the physician's secret weapon. They are the hidden ingredients in any prescription."
>
> — Norman Cousins

We have also explored the ways in which normal grief, complicated grief, and clinical depression can look and feel very similar, although there are sometimes subtle shades of gray that distinguish them.

I have recommended mourning as the essential "treatment" for grief. Mourning is not just the best way to the other side—it is the *only* way to the other side.

Yet—and this is a big YET—it is also true that if you are clinically depressed, you may not have the energy or the capacity to mourn. And if you cannot mourn, you cannot proceed. You are forever stuck. You are certainly at risk for a lifetime of unhappiness, and you may even be at risk for suicide.

And so it is sometimes also necessary for grieving people to receive biomedical treatment *in addition to meeting their six needs of mourning.*

If you:

   meet the criteria for clinical depression listed on page 33,

   AND/OR

   placed any checkmarks in the clinical depression column on page 36,

   AND/OR

   see in yourself ANY of the warning signs of suicide listed on page 42,

I want you to see a physician or therapist as soon as possible. (If you are exhibiting suicide symptoms, I want you to call a suicide hotline (see page 42), call 911, or go to the nearest emergency room *immediately.*)

Your physician or therapist will determine if you are suffering from clinical depression and if so, which type of depression. He or she will also review treatment options with you, which may include medication, herbal and dietary supplements, counseling or psychotherapy, and, in very rare cases, more extreme options such as electroconvulsive therapy or hospitalization.

Fortunately, the cultural stigma toward mental health issues is beginning to soften, and doctors and therapists work with depressed patients every single day. There is no shame in being depressed, any more than there is shame in having the flu. And treatments have been studied for many decades now and are generally considered safe and effective.

> "There's nothing, repeat, nothing to be ashamed of when you're going through a depression. If you get help, the chances of your licking it are really good. But, you have to get yourself onto a safe path."
>
> — Mike Wallace

If your depression is preventing you from making and getting to that first appointment, ask someone to help you. We all need help sometimes.

TYPES OF BIOMEDICAL TREATMENT

Antidepressants

Antidepressants are medications that influence brain activity in a way that lifts your mood. While it's not completely understood how they work, it is known that they affect neurotransmitters, which are messenger chemicals released by the nerves in your brain. These chemicals leave a nerve cell, or neuron, and travel to another neuron with the goal of communicating something. They're kind of like the Pony Express of your brain.

The messenger chemicals include serotonin, dopamine, and norepinephrine. Different antidepressants act on these chemicals differently.

Many antidepressants have been approved for use by the Food and Drug Administration for years, so there is long-term data supporting their effectiveness and safety. Doctors can't tell which particular antidepressant will help you and which won't (though your family history may offer clues; an antidepressant that has helped one member of your biological family will often work for another), so getting started on this type of medication can take some trial and error. Generally, there is a 60 to 80 percent chance that any given antidepressant will ease your symptoms.

> *"Treating the depression with drugs alone, without counseling (psychotherapy), is not only poor medicine, it is also dangerous."*
>
> — John E. Sarno, M.D.

Antidepressants don't work immediately. Patients often report that their depression starts to ease a little after two weeks, but it may take up to eight weeks for the medication to take full effect. Doctors also commonly adjust dosages to enhance effectiveness while diminishing side effects (which commonly include nausea, headache, diarrhea, insomnia, and dizziness, among other things). Antidepressants are also not without risks. Some people who take them are at increased risk for suicide. Their use should always be closely monitored by a physician.

How do antidepressants make you feel? Here are some words that patients have used to describe the sensation:

"Balanced."

"I no longer have a dark cloud hovering over me all the time."

"My emotional baseline has been lifted from miserable to neutral."

"The extreme 'uphillness' of each day has been replaced by a level field."

"I feel like myself again."

In other words, for some people, antidepressants allow them to function again. Circumstances might still make them happy or sad, but they are not deeply down and fatigued every moment of every day. For those who are grieving a loss, antidepressants can give them back the energy they need to actively express their grief.

After all, whether their depression was caused by clinical depression or by complicated grief, it was probably creating a roadblock to well being. The antidepressants opened the roadblock so they could continue on with their journey to hope and healing.

Some people take antidepressants for a period of months, while others take them for the rest of their lives. If you are prescribed antidepressants, your physician will determine the appropriate dose and duration for you.

"Through my own struggles with depression, I discovered that knowledge, therapy, medication, and education can provide the strength to get through it in one piece."

— Susan Polis Schutz

I should also note that while both therapists and physicians are trained to help patients with depression, only physicians (primary care doctors, internists, and psychiatrists) and some certified nurse practitioners can prescribe antidepressants and other medication. By the very nature of their practice, psychiatrists usually have much more experience in prescribing and monitoring antidepressants. If you have clinical depression, I urge you to find a compassionate, competent psychiatrist.

Psychotherapy/counseling

Mourning is how you heal your grief. And what is psychotherapy? It is mourning—i.e., expressing—your inner thoughts and feelings to someone who is trained to listen to you and counsel you. In fact, another term for psychotherapy is "talk therapy."

Some studies have shown that talk therapy is just as effective as antidepressants—even more effective in cases of chronic depression—at easing depression. Imaging studies in which the brains of people participating in talk therapy were scanned before and after therapy have revealed that talk therapy, like antidepressants, also physically changes the brain. So the "brain chemistry" argument for antidepressants may also, in fact, apply to talk therapy.

RESEARCH-SUPPORTED PSYCHOTHERAPIES

Scientists have evaluated only a few types of psychotherapy. The most supporting data exist for cognitive-behavior therapy and interpersonal psychotherapy, which have been shown to be effective in treating depression. Only a few studies have examined the performance of the other three therapies listed at right, but their outcomes are encouraging.

In the safety of a therapist's office, you are free to express any and all thoughts and feelings you are experiencing in your life. You can talk through your current grief, your carried grief if you have any, and your depression. You can share memories of the person who died as well as regrets, yearnings, and despairs. You can tell your stories of love and loss.

The therapist is not so much there to tell you what to do about all these thoughts and feelings as she is to listen without judging.

Depending on the type of therapy (see the list below), she may also offer suggestions for new ways of thinking and tactics for coping.

NAME OF THERAPY	APPROACH
Cognitive-behavior therapy	Teaches and encourages new behaviors to help people change overly negative thinking
	(Note: I do not believe that a strictly cognitive-behavioral approach is a good match for grief. Grief is inherently spiritual, and you cannot "think" your way through it by eliminating negative thinking. If you go to a counselor who primarily uses CBT, he may not be a good companion to you through your dark night of the soul.)
Interpersonal psychotherapy	Focuses on the social difficulties and conflicts associated with depression
Short-term psychodynamic therapy	Emphasizes understanding and correction of problematic interpersonal patterns
Client-centered therapy	Emphasizes the therapeutic potential of the therapist-client relationship (see the next page for information on "grief companioning")
Emotion-focused therapy	Builds on client-centered therapy by adding a focus on increasing

awareness of thoughts and feelings
and resolving persistent and
problematic emotional reactions

Grief companioning—a form of client-centered talk therapy

A number of years ago I realized that therapists needed a new model for caring for clients experiencing grief. Client-centered talk therapy served as a good foundation, but truly effective grief counselors thought of grief in a more holistic and spiritual way. They did not see grief as a disorder or a disease but rather as a natural and necessary process. They also did not try to "cure" their clients' grief; rather, they saw themselves as companions on the journey.

And so as I sat in the gazebo one day on the sacred grounds of the Center for Loss and Life Transition, I wrote down my core beliefs about what it means to be an effective grief counselor, and I called this new framework the Companioning Model of Grief Care. Here are its tenets:

Tenet One: Companioning is about being present to another person's pain; it is not about taking away the pain.

Tenet Two: Companioning is about going to the wilderness of the soul with another human being; it is not about thinking you are responsible for finding the way out.

Tenet Three: Companioning is about honoring the spirit; it is not about focusing on the intellect.

Tenet Four: Companioning is about listening with the heart; it is not about analyzing with the head.

Tenet Five: Companioning is about bearing witness to the struggles of others; it is not about judging or directing these struggles.

Tenet Six: Companioning is about walking alongside; it is not about leading or being led.

Tenet Seven: Companioning is about discovering the gifts of sacred silence; it does not mean filling up every moment with words.

Tenet Eight: Companioning is about being still; it is not about frantic movement forward.

Tenet Nine: Companioning is about respecting disorder and confusion; it is not about imposing order and logic.

Tenet Ten: Companioning is about learning from others; it is not about teaching them.

Tenet Eleven: Companioning is about compassionate curiosity; it is not about expertise.

While this list was written for counselors and not for grieving people, I hope it will help you understand that grief "companions," as I call them, are a unique and truly compassionate breed of counselors.

> *"I think that going into therapy is a very positive thing, and talking about it is really helpful, because the more you talk the more your fears fade, because you get it out."*
>
> — Fran Drescher

Since that time, I have trained hundreds of lay and professional grief caregivers in this philosophy. To find one near you, I invite you to call the Center for Loss at 970-226-6050. We will do our best to refer you to a caregiver who will deeply understand and honor your journey through grief. The Association of Death Education and Counseling (www.adec.org) is another good resource. On their website is a tool that will help you find a certified bereavement care specialist near you.

Combined treatment—antidepressants and talk therapy

Studies have shown that most clinically depressed patients do best when they take antidepressants and receive talk therapy at the same time. Their depressive symptoms are eased significantly more, they report better quality of life, and they are more likely to stick with their treatment program.

I have found that many physicians will prescribe antidepressants without requiring therapy, however. It is quicker and more efficient to hope that drugs alone will provide a "cure." And indeed, studies show that antidepressants alone *do* help many depressed people. Moreover, some insurance providers will cover antidepressants but not talk therapy.

However, I must re-emphasize that grief is a spiritual journey that requires expression. So if your depression has been caused at least in part by the death of someone loved or another significant loss (and I'm sure it has or you would be reading a different book on depression!), I urge you to also engage in talk therapy if you are taking antidepressants. Because though clinical depression alone may be eased by medication alone, grief will not be.

We have discussed the fact that grief gets carried when it is not mourned. So while drugs can lift the clinical depression that sometimes accompanies grief, they do not assuage the grief itself. The result can be a false sense that "everything is fine now," when actually, there is still much work to do.

If you are taking antidepressants, individual therapy is an excellent second prong in what should **always** be a two-pronged approach to treatment. Regular participation in a grief support group is another

possibility. Of course, less formal methods of grief expression—
talking to friends, journaling, participating in online forums, etc.—
are always essential, as well, but as a companion to antidepressants,
I strongly recommend individual or group counseling.

FINDING A GOOD COUNSELOR

Finding a good counselor to help you through the grief process
sometimes takes a little doing. A recommendation from someone
you trust is probably the best place to start. If he or she had a good
counseling experience and
thinks you would work well
with this counselor, then you
might want to start there.
Ultimately, though, only you
will be able to determine if a
particular counselor can help
you.

If a friend's recommendation
doesn't work out, try more
formal searching methods. Try
seeking out

- a local hospice, which may
  even have a counselor on
  staff who may be available
  to work with you;

> *"Individual psychotherapy—
> that is, engaging a distressed
> fellow human in a disciplined
> conversation and human
> relationship—requires that
> the therapist have the proper
> temperament and philosophy
> of life for such work. By that I
> mean that the therapist must
> be patient, modest, and a
> perceptive listener, rather than
> a talker and advice-giver."*
>
> — Thomas Szasz

- a self-help bereavement group, which usually maintains a list of
  counselors specializing in grief therapy;

- your personal physician, who can often refer you to bereavement
  care specialists;

- an information and referral service, such as a crisis intervention center, that maintains lists of counselors who focus on grief work;
  OR
- a hospital, family service agency, funeral home, and/or mental health clinic. All usually maintain a list of referral sources.

Depending on the size and mental health resources of your community, you may want to seek out not just a good counselor but a good grief counselor. Someone skilled at marital counseling, for example, may have little or no understanding of grief issues.

Search online for local counselors listing grief or bereavement as a specialty. Another credential to look for is certification from the Association for Death Education and Counseling (ADEC). (Go to adec.org for more information.)

Also ask the following questions during your initial consultation with the counselor:

- What are your credentials and where were you trained?
- Have you had specialized bereavement care training?
- What is your experience with grieving people?
- What is your counseling approach/recommended type of therapy with a grieving person?
- Do you have a medical consultant who assists you should I be a candidate for medication?

While I do encourage you to seek help from a compassionate grief counselor, I must also warn you that still today, many therapists work from inappropriate assumptions about the goals of grief counseling. Many project that for "successful" mourning to take place, the person must "disengage from the deceased" and "let go."

You do not need to "let go." You will not "recover" from your grief. You will not "get over it." You will not achieve "closure." You will not be "cured." Instead, a truly helpful grief counselor, or "companion," will encourage you to tell and explore your story of love and loss. She will encourage you to remember the person who died as you work to convert the relationship from one of presence to one of memory. She will help you function in the face of your depression, yes, but beyond that her main purpose will be to provide a safe place for you to mourn. She will bear witness to your pain. You will be the expert of your grief, and you will teach her what it is like for you. She will watch for signs that your grief has become complicated or your depression clinical, and in doing so, she will know if any biomedical treatment may be necessary in addition to the healing and transformative foundation of talk therapy.

Grief counselors who have been trained in my companioning philosophy (see pages 84-85) understand and work from this point of view. Others sometimes naturally adopt this basic philosophy because they are good helpers and listeners, and they have learned over the years what really helps mourners heal and what does not. But too many therapists, tainted by the medical model of grief, which says that grief is an illness that must be cured, still misunderstand their role in counseling mourners.

I encourage you to choose a counselor who understands that grief is not an illness but a normal and necessary spiritual journey. If you end up seeing a therapist who tries to help you "get over it" or tells you to "let go," it's time to find a new therapist.

IF YOUR COUNSELOR RECOMMENDS HOSPITALIZATION

Deep depression and suicidal behaviors sometimes require the intervention and safety of hospitalization. Inpatient mental health care can be very beneficial to people experiencing traumatic, complicated grief. They sometimes need to immerse themselves in intense, around-the-clock grief work to heal.

If your counselor, doctor, or another professional recommends you enter an inpatient psychiatric hospital for care, be sure to ask the following questions:

- Why should I be hospitalized?

- Which hospitals are there to choose from?

- Where can I get information on these hospitals?

- How long will I be hospitalized?

- How much does it cost?

- What if I decide against hospitalization?

Of course, less restrictive therapy options, such as outpatient counseling and support group work, should always be considered first. Many professionals feel that hospitalization is overused, and the costs can be astronomical. Yet sometimes hospitalization is the best course of action, and if this is what you need right now, don't resist the efforts being made to help you.

PART 6:

Believe in your capacity to heal

You are on a journey that is naturally frightening, extremely painful, and often lonely. Words alone cannot ease the pain you feel now. I hope, however, that this book will bring some comfort and encouragement as you make a commitment to embracing that very pain.

It takes a true commitment to heal in your grief. It takes dedication and hard work. Yes, work. The work of grief is mourning. The six needs of mourning are the tasks of your work.

> "Many of us spend our whole lives running from feeling with the mistaken belief that you cannot bear the pain. But you have already borne the pain. What you have not done is feel all you are beyond that pain."
>
> — Kahlil Gibran

SETTING YOUR INTENTION TO HEAL

With effort, commitment, and intention, your depression will ease and you will find your way back to a life of love and joy.

Commitment goes hand in hand with the concept of "setting your intention." Intention is defined as being conscious of what you want to experience. A close cousin to "affirmation," it is using the power of positive thought to produce a desired result.

> *"In the hour of adversity, be not without hope; for crystal rain falls from black clouds."*
>
> — Nizami

We often use the power of intention in our everyday lives. If you have an important presentation at work, you might focus your thoughts in the days before the presentation on speaking clearly and confidently. You might envision yourself being well-received by your colleagues. You have set your intention to succeed in this presentation. By contrast, if you focus on the many ways your presentation can fail and you succumb to your anxiety, you are much less likely to give a good presentation.

How can you use this concept in your journey through grief? By setting your intention to heal.

When you set your intention to heal, you make a true commitment to positively influence the course of your journey. You choose between being what I call a "passive witness" or an "active participant" in your grief. To heal, you must be willing to learn about the mystery of the grief journey. It can't be fixed or "resolved;" it can only be soothed and reconciled through actively experiencing the multitude of thoughts and feelings involved.

The concept of intention-setting presupposes that your outer reality is a direct reflection of your inner thoughts and beliefs. If you can change or mold some of your thoughts and beliefs, then you can influence your reality. And in journaling and speaking (and praying!)

your intentions, you help "set" them.

In part, you can choose whether you intend to experience spiritual pessimism or spiritual optimism. For example, if you believe that God is vengeful and punishes us for our sins by causing the untimely death of someone we love, it will be next to impossible for you to make it through difficult times. Not only will you carry the pain of the loss, you will carry the guilt and blame about how sinful you are to deserve this in your life. (This results in the "dirty pain" described on page 20.) By contrast, if you "set your intention" to be what I would call "spiritually optimistic" and believe that embracing the pain of your loss can lead to reconciliation, you can and will survive. (This relates to the "clean pain" described on page 20.)

RECONCILING YOUR GRIEF

An important concept to keep in mind as you journey through grief and honor your depression is that of reconciliation. You cannot "get over" or "recover from" or "resolve" your grief, but you can reconcile yourself to it. That is, you can learn to incorporate it into your consciousness and proceed with meaning and purpose in your life.

You might tell yourself, "I can and will reach out for support in my grief. I will become filled with hope that I can and will survive this loss." Together with these words, you might form mental pictures of hugging and talking to your friends and seeing your happier self in the future. Setting your intention to heal is not only a way of surviving your loss (although it is indeed that!); it is a way of guiding your grief to the best possible outcome.

Of course, you will still have to honor and embrace your pain during this time. By honoring the presence of your pain, by understanding

the appropriateness of your pain, you are committing to facing
the pain. You are committing yourself to paying attention to your
anguish in ways that allow you to begin to breathe life into your soul
again. That, my friend, is a very good reason to give attention to
your intention. The alternative would be to shut down in an effort to
avoid and deny your pain, which is to die while you are still alive.

NO REWARD FOR SPEED

Reconciling your grief does not happen quickly or efficiently. "Grief
work" may be some of the hardest work you ever do. Because
mourning is work, it calls on your physical, cognitive, emotional,
social, and spiritual energies.

Consequently, you must be patient with yourself. When you come
to trust that the pain will not last forever, it becomes tolerable.
Deceiving yourself into thinking that the pain does not even exist or
that you can avoid it only makes it intolerable. Spiritual maturity in
your grief work is attained when you embrace a paradox—to live at
once in the state of both encounter and surrender, to both "work
at" and "surrender to" your grief.

As you come to know this paradox, you will slowly discover the
soothing of your soul. Resist the need to try to figure everything
out with your head and let the paradox embrace you. You will find
yourself wrapped up in a gentle peace—the peace of living at once
in both *encounter* (your "grief work") and *surrender* (embracing the
mystery of not "understanding").

CARING FOR YOURSELF AS YOU HEAL

I remind you that the word "bereaved" means "to be torn apart"
and "to have special needs." Perhaps your most important special
need right now is to be compassionate with yourself. In fact, the

word "compassion" means "with passion." Caring for and about yourself with passion is self-compassion.

Over many years of walking with people in grief, I have discovered that most of us are hard on ourselves when we are in mourning. We judge ourselves and we shame ourselves and we take care of ourselves last. But good self-care is not only essential to your survival: it is absolutely necessary if you are to transcend your depression. To practice good self-care doesn't mean you are feeling sorry for yourself or being self-indulgent; rather, it means you are creating conditions that allow you to embrace and eventually heal the pain of your grief.

> "*I found in my research that the biggest reason people aren't more self-compassionate is that they are afraid they'll become self-indulgent. They believe self-criticism is what keeps them in line. Most people have gotten it wrong because our culture says being hard on yourself is the way to be.*"
>
> — Dr. Kristin Neff

I believe that in nurturing ourselves, in allowing ourselves the time and loving attention we need to journey safely and deeply through grief, we find meaning in our continued living. We have all heard the words, "Blessed are those who mourn, for they shall be comforted." To this I might add, "Blessed are those who learn self-compassion during times of grief, for they shall go on to discover continued meaning in life, living, and loving."

When we are torn apart, one of our most important special needs is to nurture ourselves in five important realms: physical, cognitive, emotional, social, and spiritual. Following is a brief introduction to each followed by five essential self-care tasks.

The physical realm

If you are depressed, your body is probably letting you know that it is distressed. Actually, one literal definition of the word "grievous" is "causing physical suffering." In fact, the neurotransmitters in your brain that affect your mood are the same neurotransmitters that cause physical pain. No wonder grief and physical problems are so intertwined!

> "If you don't love yourself, you cannot love others. If you have no compassion for yourself, then you are not capable of developing compassion for others."
>
> — Dalai Lama

As we have said, common physical responses to loss are troubles with sleeping and low energy. You may have difficulty getting to sleep. Perhaps even more commonly, you may wake up early in the morning and have trouble getting back to sleep. During your grief journey, your body needs more rest than usual. You may also find yourself getting tired more quickly—sometimes even at the start of the day.

Muscle aches and pains, shortness of breath, feelings of emptiness in your stomach, tightness in your throat or chest, digestive problems, sensitivity to noise, heart palpitations, queasiness, nausea, headaches, increased allergic reactions, changes in appetite, weight loss or gain, agitation, and generalized tension—these are all ways your body may react to the loss of someone loved. If you have a chronic existing health problem, it may get worse. The stress of grief can suppress your immune system and make you more susceptible to physical problems.

Did you notice that all of the physical symptoms of grief in the last paragraph can also be symptoms of depression? Once again, it is difficult—maybe impossible—to tease apart which physical problems are due to your grief and which to depression. The point is that it doesn't really matter. What matters is mourning your pain and, in the case of clinical depression (or baseline physical problems that may be preventing mourning, such as insomnia), getting treatment so that you *can* mourn.

Good self-care is paramount at this time. Your body is the house you live in. Just as your house requires care and maintenance to protect you from the outside elements, your body requires that you honor it and treat it with respect. The quality of your life ahead depends on how you take care of your body today. Try to eat nutritious foods, get regular but gentle exercise, and allow yourself to sleep when you are tired. Also try to get some sunshine each day. Many people find that low natural light levels, especially in winter, aggravate or cause depression. If you don't live where it's sunny, try a light therapy lamp.

> *"Human bodies are designed for regular physical activity. The sedentary nature of much of modern life probably plays a significant role in the epidemic incidence of depression today. Many studies show that depressed patients who stick to a regimen of aerobic exercise improve as much as those treated with medication."*
>
> — Andrew Weil

Yes, I understand that when you are depressed it's especially hard to muster the self-discipline and energy to take good care of yourself. So please, get others to help you. Schedule sessions with a personal trainer or ask a friend or neighbor to go for a walk with you every night. Buy or check out from the library audiobooks that will motivate you to walk while you listen. Splurge a little on healthy prepared foods in the deli section of a natural grocery store, or when friends ask what they can do to help, tell them you know you would benefit from better nutrition and you would welcome help with meals. Sometimes just a few small changes in physical care routines, and maybe spending a little more money where it matters, can make all the difference in preparing yourself physically to ease out of your depression.

Now is also a good time for a general check-up. Tell your healthcare provider about all of your symptoms. If she believes that any of your physical problems need treatment, she will address them. If you are not sleeping, for example, it may be impossible for you to find the energy to mourn. The "lethargy of grief" you are probably experiencing is a natural mechanism intended to slow you down and encourage you to care for your body, but until you are sleeping, little else will be possible. Antidepressants can sometimes ease physical symptoms as well.

Finally, be certain to "talk out" your grief. Many grieving people have taught me that if they avoid or repress talking about the death, their bodies will begin to express their grief for them. In addition to taking good physical care of your body, you might find that the very best thing you can do for your body right now is to care for your soul—by mourning openly and honestly.

Five physical musts

Are you doing these five things to prepare yourself physically to heal your grief and depression?

I've had a complete physical within the past year or since my loss or depression (whichever is more recent).

I walk or exercise at least 20 minutes a day, most days.

I drink eight glasses of water every day.

I eat five or more servings of fruits and vegetables each day.

I am attempting to reestablish my normal sleep patterns. I lay my body down three to four times a day for 30 minutes each time to ensure that I am getting rest. If I am struggling with insomnia or sleeping too much, I will see my primary care physician to help with this issue.

The cognitive realm

Your mind is the intellectual ability to think, absorb information, make decisions, and reason logically. Without doubt, you have special needs in the cognitive realm of your grief experience. Just as your body and emotions let you know you have experienced being "torn apart," your mind has also, in effect, been torn apart.

> "At times (grief) feels like being mildly drunk, or concussed. There is a sort of invisible blanket between the world and me. I find it hard to take in what anyone says."
>
> — C.S. Lewis

Thinking normally after a significant loss, such as the death of someone precious to you, would be very unlikely. Don't be surprised if you struggle with short-term memory problems, have trouble making even simple decisions, and think you may be "going crazy." Essentially, your mind is in a state of disorientation and confusion.

The cognitive symptoms of depression apart from grief are eerily similar. Problem-solving and higher thinking skills suffer, which can make you feel incapable of creating a plan to ease your depression.

Poor concentration and indecisiveness are also typical, as are forgetfulness, memory loss, and reduced reaction time.

Talk therapy and, if needed, antidepressants can help lessen or improve over time the cognitive symptoms of grief and depression. Now is also a good time to use administrative technologies, if you don't already. Setting reminders on your phone, for example, can help keep you on track with lots of necessary tasks. And learning centering practices, such as breathing exercises and meditation, can be a good way for you to clear your mind when you need to and proceed with the task at hand.

You also have the power of consciously revising your distorted thoughts. Earlier in this chapter I discussed the importance of "setting your intention" to mourn and heal. Your cognitive powers are quite remarkable. Willing yourself to think something can in fact help make that something come to be. Think about your desired reality and you will be moving toward making it happen.

Five cognitive musts

Are you doing these five things to prepare yourself cognitively to heal your grief and depression?

> I talk to others about my thoughts, especially those that might be obsessive or distorted, to help me distinguish clean pain from dirty pain.

> I write things down or set reminders on my phone to help me remember essential tasks.

> I use breathing exercises or meditation to help me focus.

> I have lightened my daily schedule by eliminating tasks and obligations that are not absolutely necessary right now.

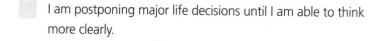 I am postponing major life decisions until I am able to think more clearly.

The emotional realm

In Part 1 we explored a multitude of emotions that are often part of normal grief. These emotions reflect that you have special needs that require support from both outside yourself and inside yourself. Befriending these emotions and practicing the self-care suggestions in this chapter can and will help you authentically mourn and heal in small doses over time. The important thing to remember is that we honor our emotions when we give attention to them.

Anhedonia is the clinical term that therapists sometimes use to describe the flatness of depression. *An* means "without" and *hedonia* means "pleasure." When you are depressed, you are living a life without pleasure. Yet even in the midst of your pain, I urge you to try to schedule, each and every day, something that would normally give you pleasure.

Often mourners need something to look forward to, a reason to get out of bed each morning. It's hard to look forward to each day when you know you will be experiencing pain and sadness. Especially when you are depressed, it can seem impossible to experience pleasure. Yet it is important for you to try. Even if it feels like you are only going through the motions at first, over time as you express your grief and perhaps receive help from a support group or skilled grief companion, the deliberate and daily practice of engaging in something pleasurable will help you begin to find and feel pleasure again. Reading, baking, going for a walk, having lunch with a friend, gardening, playing computer games—do whatever brings you enjoyment.

Exercise is also a mood-lifter. When you move your body, your brain releases "happy" chemicals such as endorphins, dopamine, and serotonin. So physical activity not only makes your body feel better, it raises your spirits.

> "Sometimes your joy is the source of your smile, but sometimes your smile can be the source of your joy."
>
> — Thich Nhat Hanh

Research has shown that helping other people is another way to counteract depression. Consider volunteering when you are ready or committing random acts of kindness, such as walking your neighbor's dog or sending an "I love you" gift to someone just because. (In fact, I dare you to set this book down right now. Rate your mood on a scale of 1 to 10, with 1 being the most depressed. Now write someone a heartfelt note of gratitude and either pop it in the mail, e-mail it, or drop it off. After you've completed this task, rate your mood again. I'll bet your mood improved, if only a little.)

Getting involved socially will also ease your depression. The challenge, of course, is that depression can be a vicious cycle. The more isolated and inactive you are, the more depressed you become, and the more depressed you become, the more isolated and inactive you grow. I understand this. But I've also said that reaching out to others for help (and accepting their help) is one of the six essential needs of mourning. So find ways to connect and let others in. You *must* if you are to live and love fully again.

Five emotional musts

Are you doing these five things to prepare yourself emotionally to heal your grief and depression?

☐ I share my emotions outside of myself. I am actively mourning.

☐ I pay attention to which activities lift my spirits, and I am making an effort to do more of those activities.

☐ I schedule at least one activity each day that I enjoy.

☐ I do not judge my emotions but instead accept and honor all of them.

☐ I am talking to others about my feelings.

The social realm

Your loss has resulted in a very real disconnection from the world around you. When you reach out to your family and friends, you are beginning to reconnect. By being aware of the larger picture, one that includes all the people in your life, you gain some perspective. You recognize you are part of a greater whole—and that recognition can empower you. You open up your heart to love again when you reach out to others. Your link to family, friends, and community is vital to your sense of well-being and belonging.

> "When we admit our vulnerability, we include others. If we deny it, we shut them out."
>
> — May Sarton

If you don't nurture the warm, loving relationships that still exist in your life, you will probably continue to feel disconnected and isolated. You may even withdraw into your own small world and grieve but not mourn. Isolation can then become the barrier that keeps your grief from softening over time. You will begin to die while you are still alive. Allow your friends and family to nurture you. Let them in, and rejoice in the connection.

Of course, you will likely find that your friendships will change during your time of grief and depression. Mourners often tell me how surprised and hurt they feel when friends fall away after a death. "I found out who my friends really are," they say. Know that just as *you* are doing your best right now, your friends are doing the best they can too. They surely still care about you, but they may also be grieving or, as if often the case, they don't know how to be present to you in your pain. Grief is awkward. They may not even be conscious of this reaction, but nonetheless, it affects their ability to support you.

> *"Do the best you can until you know better. Then when you know better, do better."*
>
> — Maya Angelou

The best way for you to respond in the face of faltering friendships or family relationships is to be proactive and honest. Even though you're the one who's grieving, you may need to be the one to phone them and keep in touch. When you talk to them, be honest. Tell them how you're really and truly feeling and that you appreciate their support. If you find that certain friends can't handle your "grief talk," stick to lighter topics with them and lean more heavily on the friends who can.

Sometimes your friends and family members can also grow fatigued by your depression. That is, they get tired of trying to help someone who always seems negative or sad. If the people in your life who are closest to you are expressing impatience with your grief or depression, take that as a cue to seek social support from a support group and/or a grief counselor. They are not necessarily doing anything wrong, and neither are you. It may simply be that you need more help than they can offer right now, and that's OK. There are others who can and will help you.

You may be lucky enough to find one particular friend or family member who will stick by your side and listen to and support you. Sometimes this person is someone who has also experienced a significant loss or major depression. Though no one else will grieve this loss just like you, there are often many others who have had similar experiences. We are rarely totally alone on the path of mourning. Even when there is no guide, there are fellow travelers.

If you connect with a "grief buddy," consider making a pact to call each other whenever one of you needs to talk. Promise to listen without judgment. Commit to spending time together. You might arrange to meet once a week for breakfast or lunch, for example.

Finally, consider reaching out to connect socially with people with similar spiritual beliefs. If you are a follower of a certain religion, now is the time to look into support groups and other services at your place of worship. Non-religious spiritual groups sometimes meet at meditation or community centers. You may find that fellow spiritual seekers will not only help you explore your grief but also provide you with a much-needed social network right now.

Five social musts

Are you doing these five things to prepare yourself socially to heal your grief and depression?

- I am being honest with others about what I am thinking and feeling.

- I am reaching out for help, and I am accepting help when it is offered to me.

- I am having grace with those friends and family members who seem unable to support me right now and turning to those who can.

I am honoring my natural need to withdraw right now, but I am not isolating myself too much.

I am looking into or connecting with new social groups—especially those comprised of fellow travelers on this journey through loss, grief, and depression.

The spiritual realm

When you are torn apart, you may have many spiritual questions for which there are no easy answers: Is there a God? Why me? Will life ever be worth living again? That is why, if I could, I would encourage all of us when we are in the midst of grief to put down "Nurture my spirit" first on our daily to-do lists.

I believe that grief is first and foremost a spiritual journey, and therefore the depression of grief is a spiritual experience. When you are depressed you are often wrestling with deeply spiritual and existential questions. The depression necessarily slows you down and makes you turn inward so that you will give these questions the time and attention they deserve.

> "In order to experience everyday spirituality, we need to remember that we are spiritual beings spending some time in a human body."
>
> — Barbara de Angelis

We tend to think of spirituality as uplifting and positive, but the truth is that spirituality can be deeply challenging and depressing. As Carl Jung said, "Filling the conscious mind with ideal conceptions is a characteristic of Western theosophy, but not the confrontation with the shadow and the world of darkness. One does not become enlightened by imagining figures of light, but by making the darkness conscious."

Yes, spirituality presents the biggest challenges but also promises the greatest rewards. Finding ways to actively engage your spirituality right now will help you mourn and heal.

You can discover spiritual understanding in many ways and through many practices—prayer, worship, and meditation among them. You can nurture your spirituality in many places—nature, church, temple, mosque, monastery, retreat center, and kitchen table among them. No one can "give" you spirituality from the outside in. Even when you gain spiritual understanding from a specific faith tradition, the understanding is yours alone, discovered through self-examination, reflection, and spiritual transformation.

If you attend a place of worship, visit it often in the coming weeks either for services or an informal time of prayer and solitude. If you don't have a place of worship, perhaps you have a friend who seems spiritually grounded. Ask her how she learned to nurture her spirituality. Sometimes, someone else's ideas and practices provide just what you need to stimulate your own spiritual self-care.

Consider starting each new day with meditation or prayer. When you wake up, stretch before getting out of bed. Feel the blood coursing through your body. Listen to the hum of your consciousness. Repeat a simple phrase or prayer to yourself, such as: "Today I will live and love fully. Today I will appreciate my life." You might also offer words of gratitude: "Thank you, God, for giving me this day. Help me to appreciate it and to make it count."

I also suggest you start keeping a gratitude journal. Each night before you go to bed, recount your blessings from the day. At first you may find this challenging, but as you continue this daily practice, it will get easier and more joyful. Think of all you have to be thankful for. This is not to deny you your overwhelming loss and the need to mourn. However, you are being self-compassionate when you consider the things that make your life worth living, too. Reflect on your possibilities for joy and love each day. Honor those possibilities and have gratitude for them. Be grateful for your physical health and your beautiful spirit. Be grateful for your family and friends and the concern of strangers. Above all, be grateful for this very moment. When you are grateful, you prepare the way for inner peace.

For me, spirituality involves a sense of connection to all things in nature, God, and the world at large. I recognize that, for some, contemplating a spiritual life in the midst of the pain of grief can be difficult. Yet life is a miracle, and we need to remind ourselves of that, during both happy times and sad times. When it comes to our spiritual lives, we have an abundance of choices, all of which can be doors leading to the soul. Spirituality can be found in simple things: a sunrise or sunset; the unexpected kindness of a stranger; the rustle of the wind in the trees.

If you have doubts about your capacity to connect with God and the world around you, try to approach the world with the openness of a child. Embrace the pleasure that comes from the simple sights, smells, and sounds that greet your senses. You can and will find yourself rediscovering the essentials within your soul and the spirit of the world around you.

Nurturing a spiritual life invites you to connect with nature and the people around you. Your heart opens and your life takes on renewed meaning and purpose. You are filled with compassion for other people, particularly those who have come to know grief and depression. You become kinder, gentler, more forgiving of others as well as yourself.

Five spiritual musts

Are you doing these five things to prepare yourself spiritually to heal your grief and depression?

I allow myself to search for meaning and reconsider my spiritual beliefs and practices.

I am connecting with my faith community if I find it helpful, and I am exploring other faith and spiritual communities if I am interested.

I express my spirituality daily.

I spend time in nature as often as I can.

I make it a point to express gratitude in some way every day.

HOW RECONCILIATION FEELS

As you embrace your sadness, meet your six needs of mourning, and care for yourself, ever so slowly and gradually you will sense that you are making progress in healing your depression. You will begin to feel reconciliation unfold. You will recognize that life is and will continue to be different than it was before your loss. We, as human beings, never "get over" or resolve our grief, but instead become reconciled to it. We come to reconciliation in our grief journeys when the full reality of the death becomes a part of us.

> *"If I had not already been meditating, I would certainly have had to start. I've treated my own depression for many years with exercise and meditation, and I've found that to be a tremendous help."*
>
> — Judy Collins

Beyond an intellectual working through of the death, there is also an emotional and spiritual working through. What had been understood at the "head" level is now understood at the "heart" level.

> "Pain becomes bearable when we are able to trust that it won't last forever, not when we pretend it doesn't exist."
>
> — Alla Bozarth-Campbell

You will find that as you achieve reconciliation, the sharp, ever-present pain of grief will give rise to a renewed sense of meaning and purpose. Your feelings of loss will not completely disappear, yet they will soften, and the intense pangs of grief will become less frequent. Hope for a continued life will emerge as you are able to make commitments to the future, realizing that the person you have given love to and received love from will never be forgotten. The unfolding of this journey is not intended to create a return to an "old normal" but instead the discovery of a "new normal."

To help you explore where you are in your movement toward reconciliation, the following signs of healing may be helpful. You don't have to meet each of these criteria for healing to be taking place. Again, remember that reconciliation is an ongoing process. If you are early in the work of mourning, you may not meet any of these criteria. But this list will give you a way to monitor your progress.

As you embrace your grief and do the work of mourning, you will begin to notice

• a recognition of the reality and finality of the death.

• a return to stable eating and sleeping patterns.

- a renewed sense of release from the person who died or the loss. You will have thoughts about the person, but you will not be preoccupied by these thoughts.

- the capacity to once again enjoy experiences in life that are normally enjoyable.

- the establishment of new and healthy relationships.

- the capacity to live a full life without feelings of guilt or lack of self-worth.

- the drive to organize and plan your life toward the future.

- the serenity to become comfortable with the way things are rather than attempting to make things as they were.

- the versatility to welcome more change in your life.

- the awareness that you have allowed yourself to fully grieve, and you have survived.

- the awareness that you do not "get over" your grief; instead, you have a new reality, meaning, and purpose in your life.

- the acquaintance of new parts of yourself that you have discovered in your grief journey.

- the adjustment to new role changes that have resulted from the loss of the relationship.

- the acknowledgment that the pain of loss in an inherent part of life resulting from the ability to give and receive love.

Usually we don't check our lawns daily to see if the grass is growing, but it does grow, and soon we come to realize it's time to mow the grass again. Likewise, we don't look at ourselves each day as

CLOSURE: A MISNOMER

Sometimes well-intentioned but misinformed people will ask you that dreaded question, "Do you have closure?" Sometimes they will phrase it differently, asking, "Are you over it?" or "Have you let go?"

Without doubt, you will have someone, with seeming great authority, tell you that if you haven't put your grief and mourning behind you, you aren't really trying to achieve "closure." Keep in mind what Shakespeare once observed: "Everyone can master grief but he that has it."

Webster's Dictionary defines closure as "finished, ended." Yet in my thirty-plus years of companioning thousands of people in grief, and in my own personal loss experiences, I have come to realize that closure is often a projected goal of those who have never walked the walk.

Grief never ends, and you are a different person after the loss than you were before the loss. There is no closing, there is only journeying. So, transformation ("an entire change in form"), YES. Closure ("finished, ended"), NO! When someone asks you if you have "closure," do remember to have grace, for they know not what they do.

mourners to see how we are healing. Yet we do come to realize, over the course of months and years, that we have come a long way. We have taken some important steps toward healing our wounds and moving from soul work to spirit work.

Usually there is not one great moment of "arrival" but instead subtle changes and small advancements. It's helpful to have gratitude for even very small gains. We often move forward in ways we do not even understand, through the quiet workings of grace. When we get there we are never sure how it happened—that is part of the mystery! If you are beginning to taste your food again, be thankful. If you mustered the energy to meet your friend for lunch, be grateful. If you finally got a good night's sleep, rejoice.

One of my greatest teachers, C. S. Lewis, wrote in *A Grief Observed* about his grief symptoms as they eased in his journey to reconciliation:

> There was no sudden, striking, and emotional transition.
> Like the warming of a room or the coming of daylight,
> when you first notice them they have already been going on
> for some time.

Of course, you will take some steps backward from time to time, but that is to be expected. Keep believing in yourself. Set your intention to reconcile your grief and have hope that you can and will come to experience happiness and joy and life and love again.

Realistically, even though you have hope for your healing, you should not expect it to happen overnight, particularly if you have been challenged by clinical depression or complicated grief. Many grieving people think that it should and, as a result, experience a loss of self-confidence and self-esteem that leaves them questioning their capacity to heal. If this is the situation for you, keep in mind that you are not alone.

> *"Only people who are capable of loving strongly can also suffer great sorrow, but this same necessity of loving serves to counteract their grief and heals them."*
>
> — Leo Tolstoy

You may find that a helpful procedure is to take inventory of your own timetable expectations for reconciliation. Ask yourself questions like, "Am I expecting myself to heal more quickly than is humanly possible? Have I mistakenly given myself a specific deadline for when I should be 'over' my grief?" Recognize that you may be hindering your own healing by expecting too much of yourself. Take your healing one day at a time. It will ultimately allow you to move toward and rediscover continued meaning in your life.

You can't control death or ignore your human need to mourn when it impacts your life. You do, however, have the choice to help yourself heal. Embracing the pain of your grief is probably one of the hardest jobs you will ever do. As you do this work, surround yourself with compassionate, loving people who are willing to "walk with" you.

THE TRANSFORMATIVE NATURE OF GRIEF

Grief is a spiritual, transformative journey. I'm certain you have discovered that you have been changed by your loss. Many mourners have said to me, "I have grown from this experience. I am a different person."

Now, don't take me the wrong way. Believe me, I understand that the growth resulted from something you would have preferred to avoid. While I have come to believe that our greatest gifts often come from our wounds, these are not wounds we masochistically go looking for. When others offer untimely comments like, "You'll grow from this," your right to be hurt, angry, or deeply sad is taken away from you.

Yet you are changing and growing nevertheless as a result of this loss. We as human beings can't help but be forever changed by the love and the death of someone in our lives. You may discover that you have developed new attitudes. You may be more patient or more sensitive to the feelings and circumstances of others, especially those suffering from loss. You may have new insights that guide the way you live your new life. You may have developed new skills or ways of viewing humankind or the world around you.

Your transformation probably also involves exploring your assumptions about life. Death invites this type of exploration. Your loss experiences have a tendency to transform your values and priorities. Every loss in life calls out for a new search for meaning, including a natural struggle with spiritual concerns, often transforming your vision of your God and your faith life.

Finally, your transformation may well include a need to do and be all you can be. In some ways, death loss seems to free the potential within. Questions such as "Who am I? What am I meant to do with my life?" often naturally arise during grief. Answering them inspires a hunt. You may find yourself searching for your very soul.

Yes, sorrow is an inescapable dimension of our human experience. We love and so we grieve. We rejoice and then we suffer. And in our suffering, we are transformed. While it hurts to suffer lost love, the alternative is apathy, or the inability to suffer, and it results in a lifestyle that avoids human relationships to avoid suffering.

You have many choices in living the transformation that grief has brought to your life. You can choose to visualize your heart opening each and every day. When your heart is open, you are receptive to what life brings you, both happy and sad. By staying open and present, you create a gateway to your healing.

When this happens you will know that the long nights of suffering in the wilderness have given way to a journey toward the dawn. You will know that new life has come as you celebrate the first rays of a new light and new beginning.

HOPE FOR YOUR HEALING

I think about the man I was honored to companion following the tragic death of his seven-year-old son, Adam, in a car accident. He was heartbroken. His soul was darkened. He had to come to know the deepest despair. Yet, he discovered that if he were to ever live again, he would have to work *through* his grief. So, he adopted the mantra, "Work on!"

In his process of conscious intention-setting, he decided to believe that even the most heart-wrenching loss can be survived. Perhaps refusing to give in to despair is the greatest act of hope and faith.

Yes, you go to the wilderness, you cry out in the depths of your despair. Darkness may seem to surround you. But rising up within you is the profound awareness that the pain of the grief is a sign of having given and received love.

And where the capacity to love and be loved, to give happiness and be happy, has been before, it can be again.

Living in the present moment of your pain while having hope for a good that is yet to come are not mutually exclusive. Actually, hoping and even anticipating can deepen your experience of the moment and motivate you to "work on!"

"The pain passes, but the beauty remains."

— Pierre Auguste Renoir

Coming out of the darkness of depression is within your grasp if you use the ideas in this book to create an action plan for your body, mind, and spirit. A main purpose of life is to practice compassion toward all human beings, including ourselves. The important thing to remember with depression is to feel compassion for yourself and seek the help you both need and deserve. Your depression, while painful and even frightening, is a sign that aspects of your life need attention. By reading this book, you have taken an important first step. Congratulations!

I hope this little book has helped you during your time of great sadness. Most of all, I hope it has helped you understand your needs to mourn and reach out to others. Whether you are experiencing normal grief, clinical depression, complicated grief, or a combination of these, you need and deserve the companionship of empathetic friends and helpers. Trained professionals can also determine if you might benefit from antidepressants or other therapies.

Always remember: Darkness is the chair upon which light sits.

I wish you good grief and Godspeed.

Glossary of terms

anhedonia	the inability to experience pleasure from things that normally give you pleasure
carried grief	grief from earlier in life that was never mourned
clean pain	the normal and necessary hurt of loss
clinical depression	depression characterized by a depressed mood and/or lack of pleasure as well as other symptoms, particularly a low sense of self-worth and the inability to function day-to-day
companioning	my philosophy of grief counseling; the art of walking alongside someone in grief
complicated grief	normal grief that has strayed off course and is not softening over time but instead becoming entrenched or worsening
dirty pain	the compounding or distorting of the hurt of loss by worrying about "what ifs" or catastrophizing
divine spark	your soul or essence
dosing your pain	embracing your hurt a bit at a time, allowing yourself to retreat and take a break before you approach it again
grief	what you think and feel inside yourself when you experience a loss
liminal space	the place you are when you are in transition or between comfortable situations
mourning	expressing your grief outside yourself
perturbation	when you embrace, explore, and express your feelings, which allows them to change and soften; your emotions in motion
reconciliation	when you have integrated your grief into your life and are able to once again live and love fully

Training and Speaking Engagements

To contact Dr. Wolfelt about speaking engagements or training opportunities at his Center for Loss and Life Transition, email him at DrWolfelt@centerforloss.com.

The Journey Through Grief
Reflections on Healing
SECOND EDITION

Quotations by A. Wolfelt on pages 52-62 are excerpted from this book.

This revised, second edition of *The Journey Through Grief* takes Dr. Wolfelt's popular book of reflections and adds space for guided journaling, asking readers thoughtful questions about their unique mourning needs and providing room to write responses.

The Journey Through Grief is organized around the six needs that all mourners must yield to—indeed embrace—if they are to go on to find continued meaning in life and living. Following a short explanation of each mourning need is a series of brief, spiritual passages that, when read slowly and reflectively, help mourners work through their unique thoughts and feelings.

"The reflections in this book encourage you to think, yes, but to think with your heart and soul," writes Dr. Wolfelt. "They invite you to go to that spiritual place inside you and, transcending our mourning-avoiding society and even your own personal inhibitions about grief, enter deeply into the journey."

ISBN 978-1-879651-11-1 • 152 pages • hardcover • $21.95

ALL DR. WOLFELT'S PUBLICATIONS CAN BE ORDERED BY MAIL FROM

Companion Press
3735 Broken Bow Road | Fort Collins, CO 80526
(970) 226-6050 | www.centerforloss.com

Understanding Your Grief

TEN ESSENTIAL TOUCHSTONES FOR FINDING HOPE AND HEALING YOUR HEART

One of North America's leading grief educators, Dr. Alan Wolfelt has written many books about healing in grief. This book is his most comprehensive, covering the essential lessons that mourners have taught him in his three decades of working with the bereaved.

In compassionate, down-to-earth language, *Understanding Your Grief* describes ten touchstones—or trail markers—that are essential physical, emotional, cognitive, social, and spiritual signs for mourners to look for on their journey through grief.

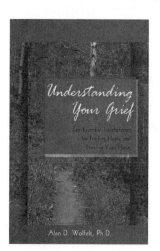

The Ten Essential Touchstones:
1. Open to the presence of your loss.
2. Dispel misconceptions about grief.
3. Embrace the uniqueness of your grief.
4. Explore your feelings of loss.
5. Recognize you are not crazy.
6. Understand the six needs of mourning.
7. Nurture yourself.
8. Reach out for help.
9. Seek reconciliation, not resolution.
10. Appreciate your transformation.

Think of your grief as a wilderness—a vast, inhospitable forest. You must journey through this wilderness. To find your way out, you must become acquainted with its terrain and learn to follow the sometimes hard-to-find trail that leads to healing. In the wilderness of your grief, the touchstones are your trail markers. They are the signs that let you know you are on the right path. When you learn to identify and rely on the touchstones, you will find your way to hope and healing.

ISBN 978-1-879651-35-7 • 176 pages • softcover • $14.95

ALL DR. WOLFELT'S PUBLICATIONS CAN BE ORDERED BY MAIL FROM

Companion Press
3735 Broken Bow Road | Fort Collins, CO 80526
(970) 226-6050 | www.centerforloss.com

The Understanding Your Grief Journal

EXPLORING THE TEN ESSENTIAL TOUCHSTONES

Writing can be a very effective form of mourning, or expressing your grief outside yourself. And it is through mourning that you heal in grief.

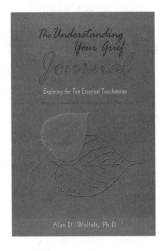

The Understanding Your Grief Journal is a companion workbook to *Understanding Your Grief*. Designed to help mourners explore the many facets of their unique grief through journaling, this compassionate book interfaces with the ten essential touchstones. Throughout, journalers are asked specific questions about their own unique grief journeys as they relate to the touchstones and are provided with writing space for the many questions asked.

Purchased as a set together with *Understanding Your Grief*, this journal is a wonderful mourning tool and safe place for those in grief. It also makes an ideal grief support group workbook.

ISBN 978-1-879651-38-5 • 112 pages • softcover • $14.95

ALL DR. WOLFELT'S PUBLICATIONS CAN BE ORDERED BY MAIL FROM

Companion Press
3735 Broken Bow Road | Fort Collins, CO 80526
(970) 226-6050 | www.centerforloss.com

Living in the Shadow of the Ghosts of Grief: Step into the Light

RECONCILE OLD LOSSES AND OPEN THE DOOR TO INFINITE JOY AND LOVE

Are you depressed? Anxious? Angry? Do you have trouble with trust

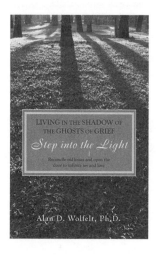

and intimacy? Do you feel a lack of meaning and purpose in your life? You may well be living in the shadow of the ghosts of grief.

When you suffer a loss of any kind—whether through abuse, divorce, job loss, the death of someone loved or other transitions—you naturally grieve inside. To heal your grief, you must express it. That is, you must mourn your grief. If you don't, you will carry your grief into your future, and it will undermine your happiness for the rest of your life.

This compassionate guide will help you learn to identify and mourn your carried grief so you can go on to live the joyful, whole life you deserve.

ISBN 978-1-879651-51-7 • 160 pages • softcover • $13.95

ALL DR. WOLFELT'S PUBLICATIONS CAN BE ORDERED BY MAIL FROM

Companion Press
3735 Broken Bow Road I Fort Collins, CO 80526
(970) 226-6050 I www.centerforloss.com

Healing Your Grieving Heart

100 PRACTICAL IDEAS

When someone loved dies, we must express our grief if we are to heal. In other words, we must mourn. But knowing what to do with your grief and how to mourn doesn't always come naturally in our mourning-avoiding culture.

This book offers 100 practical ideas to help you practice self-compassion. Some of the ideas teach you the principles of grief and mourning. The remainder offer practical, action-oriented tips for embracing your grief. Each also suggests a *carpe diem*, which will help you seize the day by helping you move toward healing today.

ISBN 978-1-879651-25-8
128 pages • softcover • $11.95

ALL DR. WOLFELT'S PUBLICATIONS CAN BE ORDERED BY MAIL FROM

Companion Press
3735 Broken Bow Road I Fort Collins, CO 80526
(970) 226-6050 I www.centerforloss.com

Eight Critical Questions for Mourners...

AND THE ANSWERS THAT WILL HELP YOU HEAL

When loss enters your life, you are faced with many choices. The questions you ask and the choices you make will determine whether you become among the "living dead" or go on to live until you die. If you are going to integrate grief into your life, it helps to recognize what questions to ask yourself on the journey.

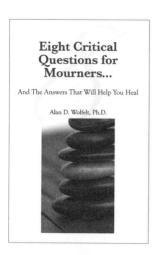

Eight Critical Questions for Mourners...

And The Answers That Will Help You Heal

Alan D. Wolfelt, Ph.D.

1. Will I grieve or mourn this loss?

2. Will I befriend my feelings of loss, or will I inhibit them?

3. Will I be a passive witness or an active participant in my grief?

4. Will I embrace the uniqueness of my grief?

5. Will I work on the six needs of mourning, or will I fall victim to the cliché "time heals all wounds"?

6. Will I believe I must achieve resolution, or will I work toward reconciliation?

7. Will I embrace my transformation?

8. Will this loss add to my "divine spark," or will it take away my life force?

This book provides the answers that will help you clarify your experiences and encourage you to make choices that honor the transformational nature of grief and loss.

ISBN 978-1-879651-62-3 • 176 pages • softcover • $18.95

ALL DR. WOLFELT'S PUBLICATIONS CAN BE ORDERED BY MAIL FROM

Companion
PRESS

Companion Press
3735 Broken Bow Road | Fort Collins, CO 80526
(970) 226-6050 | www.centerforloss.com